From Persia to Puerto Rico

## saga of an Iranian boy

By Yigal Yomtov

**New Generation Publishing**

# REVIEWS

- By Spencer Shaw **Jewpro**
  *Thoroughly, enjoyable and a must read to get an insight about Iran and Iranians. Would recommend it. -   August 2013*

- By Simon Yaffe, **Jewish telegraph**
  *How cultural difference in Iran, Israel, and United States affected the life of a boy in search of America America. -   August 2013*

- By Emb Hashmi Senior Correspondent of **Asian World news**
  *An Iranian boy finds heaven in Puerto Rico
  –   August   2013*

- By Mona Zarei, **University of Miami**
  *"Enjoyed it so much. Had to read it twice" -Nov 2013*

- By **Dr. Ralph Zagha, M.D., P.A. Urologic Surgery**
  *An enjoyable read - October 2013*

- By **Mark Soloway, MD Chief, Urologic Oncology Memorial Physician Group Division of Urology**
  *If you want a Magic Carpet ride to Iran as it was between 1945-19xx as navigated by a wonderful storyteller then read Yigal's personal account in his entertaining and most informative book "From Persia to Puerto Rico*

# Foreword

I have been reliving my life in my head for the past 12 years. Since 2002, I have felt the need to put it down in writing, to share what I have seen, experienced, and lived. Yet, there was always the fear that some would be insulted by my retelling of these stories. Others may feel a deep, defensive-patriotism to the countries that have touched my life. Those same countries that raised me, fed me, educated me: their political, social, and religious climates shaped my life. Those same countries that I simultaneously love and criticize.

It wasn't until 2010 that I was finally able to organize and calm my thoughts and memories just enough to put on paper the sequence of stories that together tell of my life in Iran, Israel, Colombia, and the U.S. including Puerto Rico.

Although English is not my mother tongue, at my request, there has been limited editing so that the reader may feel as if he/she were sitting next to me, hearing my story, in my voice. What you are about to read is the truth.

This book is dedicated to my Daughter Galia who supported me in every step of this endeavor. It is equally dedicated to all those who believe in fairness and justice.

# Chapter 1

# The night I was shot at

# Chapter 1

## The night I was shot at

December 28 1998, Luquillo, Puerto Rico about 9 PM

"Esto es un asalto cabron!" the man shouted at me. It had
been a rainy evening. Suddenly I heard a sound from
outside of the farm house, in front of the rainforest. I
went out to investigate as to what had happened. The back
window of my Toyota was broken. As I approached the
gate an assailant came out of hiding behind the huge pine
tree about six feet away. I could barely see his goatee and
the metal part of his pistol in the dim moonlight. Before I
got a chance, he pointed the gun at me, with a strong voice
saying,
"Esto es un asalto cabron!" (This is a stick up, bustard)
    It is amazing how many things pass through one's
mind within seconds in a desperate situation as such. In a
split second, I thought he would kill me even if I
surrendered. It was at that moment that I told him to "Go
to hell" and turned around running in a zigzag manner
towards the house while he took a shot.
    A bullet hit the left window of my car, but I was
safely inside. I started screaming the name of my only
neighbor a hundred feet away till he finally showed up
and I felt safe. After shaking and palpitations for hours,
suddenly my childhood in Esfahan, Iran passed before my
eyes.
    The first thing I remembered was when I was about
five and a half when my mother took me to the Jewish
Kindergarten. The female teacher would teach us

7

Jewish stories as well as reading and writing Farsi and Arithmetic. She would hit us on the palm of our hands with her wooden ruler if we didn't pay attention while she taught. I dreaded going to Kinder so early in the morning during the cold winter days.

We were three families living in my grandfather's house. Our source of heat during the winter was a cement square hole in the middle of the room which was filled with hot carbon coals covered by a four legged table and then covered by a handmade blanket. We would all get under the blanket covering ourselves up to the chest.

Our drinking water was drawn from a deep well located in a corner of the house. Our parents would throw a pail attached to the end of a long rope, pulling it up once was filled with water.

I don't remember much more from this period except the fact that my mother was a stern parent and already had expectations of seeing me as a brilliant student at any cost.

At seven, I was enrolled in the Jewish Elementary School, which had taken a hundred years of efforts to come into existence. The wealthy French Jewish Rothschild family together with Adolphe Crémieux (founder of Alliance Israelite Universelle) had been trying to help the Jews of the Middle East with an education system since the eighteen hundreds. The Gajar rulers of Iran were wined and dined by the Rothschilds whenever they were in Paris for fun and gambling. At one of these meetings with the Gajar ruler of the time, Naser Oldin Shah was so overwhelmed by Rothschild's generosity that he suggested the family should buy a country for the Jews. But that was just a dream. Once the Rothschild family had the green light to help the Jews, they came to Iran, and within some years, each Iranian major city had a Jewish primary

School. They were all called the same name, "Etehad," which means Unity in Farsi. The organization behind it was Alliance. Thanks to the Rothschild family and later the American Joint, 98% in our ghetto ended up as professionals.

I had to be up by 6 AM and ready to leave for school by 7 AM. From age seven we would go to school unaccompanied—a distance of about three miles—and we were targeted for harassment by some Muslim boys once we left the ghetto.

The first time a Muslim boy called me a "dirty Jew," being seven years old, I could not comprehend why he called me dirty. After all, we had to wash our hands and face every morning even in the blistering cold. To get to school, one had to cross the ghetto since our school was located in a totally Muslim area.

Our ghetto was straight out of the Babylonian structure of poor people. Houses were mostly made of mud: one attached to another in dark alleys with dirt roads. When it rained, roads would become a pool of mud. In the center of the ghetto you had synagogues as well as stores. Almost all stores were owned and run by Muslims except the kosher butcheries. Even the Jewish public bath was owned by Muslims. The butchers would leave the ghetto by 4 AM accompanied by a "Shochet" (a religious Jew who had studied all the laws concerning the conditions of permitted animals before and during slaughtering). They would buy mostly sheep, which were then slaughtered by the Shochet. Should any of the animal organs have a blemish, the animal had to be disposed of or sold to non-Jews at a great loss. That is one of the reasons why kosher meat has always been rather expensive.

The Jewish public bath was devoted to men from 5 AM to 9 AM and afterwards was used by women. My father would wake me up at 5 AM once every two weeks to go to the bath. It was crying time from home to bath. This went on till I was ten, when the same organization which helped with schooling rented the public bath on Fridays for students free of charge.

I could hardly wait for Friday, which is the Muslim Sabbath and our day off from school. Being in a Jewish school, we had both Friday and Saturday off. Friday mornings I would accompany my mother to the main square of the ghetto where she would buy a live chicken from Muslim peasant women and have it slaughtered by a Shochet right then and there. It wasn't a pleasant sight to see the chicken running and bleeding to death. Before sun down, my grandfather, a towering man, 6.2 feet tall, would hold my hand, taking me to the big synagogue for prayers.

He was well known for being a leader and even more for having two thumbs, one attached to the other on his right hand. In fact, his nickname was Jacob the Six Finger. I still fondly remember late summers when he would buy ripe grapes, put them in a huge pot and have me step on them in his preparation of wine making. He always made his own wine, of which he enjoyed a cup nightly. On our way to the Sabbath and Sabbath prayers was another phenomenon, deserving to be written as a book on its own.

Our ghetto had its own share of crazy people. In fact, we had several locos. But here are a few of most mentionable. Isaac the Loco was a poor low-wit man, half blind, and with a visible hernia. He would put his hand on your head, recite a blessing (which he didn't know well) for the equivalent of a penny. Next was Simon, whose wife had left him for another, which drove him to madness. All day long he would curse his brother in law rhythmically. Simon held him responsible for the loss of his wife; he had gone truly mad.

I even saw him hit a crooked tree, telling it to straighten up.

Then there was Sarah the Mad, who would hold the whole world responsible for her prince having left her. In fact, she had never been married and was mad from her youth.

My mother would make sure that on Fridays I was cleaned and dressed (I had a clean shirt and ironed pants only for Saturdays). Sabbath starts at sundown on Friday, and is observed till Saturday night. My mother suffered constantly from lack of money since she had married my father, who was from a lower class. She had to; when a young girl became orphan as my mother did at age two, she lost all privileges. If a girl lost her father, her social standing would be considered that of an orphan. She would become quite valueless and even looked down upon. With no dowry, a fatherless girl offered no value to prospective grooms and their families. Thus, although she was from a prominent family, no one of her class would marry her. She would fight my father until I got a shirt or a pair of pants. When he would finally give up, he would take his old suit to the street of Jewish tailors and have a tailor open the suit and make me clothing with whatever material he could save from the old suit. We slept on a thin mattress on the floor and whenever a pair of pants needed ironing, she would fold the pants and put them under her mattress overnight whereby her weight would iron the pants.

My grandparents' house, where we lived, was a rectangular house. Rooms were built all around a large central courtyard. My grandparents used one room; we had two with my uncle, his wife and four daughters in another two. There was a common huge kitchen and a main room with stained glass windows which was reserved for Saturday lunches after returning from the

Synagogue. There were pomegranate trees around the courtyard garden and a huge vine with which my Grandpa would make a Sukkah for the festival of Tabernacle, or Sukkoth. Our water was drawn from a scary well in a corner of the house. Scary because we would often hear how a child fell in a well and died. During the season, we would pick the pomegranates while squeezing them all around till the skin became soft to the touch, then we would make a small hole with our teeth, enjoying the most delicious juice ever.

All dressed, my Grandpa, my Agachi, would take me by hand on our way to the Friday night prayers. If at times we were early, you could still see Muslim fisherman (they would come to the ghetto every Friday afternoon to sell us fish since it was an integral part of Sabbath meals). They would approach us with whatever fish was left, trying to exchange fish for wine. Agachi would simply smile and wish them well.

Often, our Sabbath meals would end up in a fight between my mother and my aunt - uncle's wife. My mother had sons while she had only daughters; in time four of them. This caused great jealousy and enough reason to dislike my mother. A woman was very downgraded if she had no sons. In fact, at times, they were divorced by the husband hoping that he could have sons if he married another woman.

Saturdays were boring and restful. We were not permitted to do much except read Torah and listen to Jewish religious wisdom. We were taught from an early age that striking a match on the Sabbath would be the surest and shortest way to Hell. As a result, my mother used to pay a few rials to a neighboring Muslim to come and light our kerosene stove, to warm up food on Saturdays. We called him/her the Sabbath Goy, or Saturday's Gentile.

Children had to beg for months for entertainment, Until Saturday night, after Sabbath was over, when you could see at least three stars in the sky, our parents would take us out of the ghetto in the Chehar Bagh, or Four Gardens. Chehar Bagh was and still is one of the nicest and widest boulevards in the world. It was built during the reign of the Great King Abbas of Safavid dynasty over five hundred years ago. It is truly a sight. So much so that the English Lord Byron wrote "Esfahan nesfe jahan," which translated from Farsi simply means "Esfahan in half of the world." He wrote this when he saw the boulevard and the breath-taking mosques built in the same era. There is a strong belief that the famous Champs Elysees of Paris was designed after the Chehar Bagh.

My mother would fill our pockets with home roasted nuts and we would be on our way. Once out of the ghetto, some Muslims would give us a sarcastic smile and chant with a Jewish accent in Farsi, "Jews are going to have fun." All in all this was as far as they would go. More malicious acts were reserved for Sunday morning, first day of the school week, on our way to school.

After about three miles, you would get to Meidan Shah, or Shah's Square. Again, by far one of the largest city squares in the world. There is no way that one can give it justice just by writing about it. It is a square surrounded by immense arches with carved out hollow images of musical instruments all over them. On its north you have the gate to the famous bazaar where you could buy simply anything you need. On the south, there is Masjid Shah. The east end is occupied by the palaces of King Abbas and the west enjoys having Sheikh Lotfolah Masjid, which was made for the women and female relatives of King Abbas. Its turquoise entrance would leave anyone breathless.

Continuing on the way to Chehar Bagh you would pass the street of bicycle shops; the dream of every young boy. After Amsterdam, it was a known fact that Esfahan was number two city in numbers of bicycles. When a boy finished elementary school, he would be blessed with a bicycle, not out of the kindness of his parents' hearts but simply because it was the cheapest way of transportation.

Now we finally enter the boulevard. It was vast. It had two huge cement lanes; two lanes for bicycles and a pedestrian mid-section about fifty feet wide. Both sides of the boulevard were jam packed with stores: clothing, shoes, home goods, bakeries, restaurants, cinemas, Chai Khane (tea houses), dry goods, and other foods of all kinds. It would take hours to walk the wide avenue on both sides and yet this was the greatest pastime of the Esfahani people every night. 99% of those that came out were men, of course.

Once on this boulevard, we were transplanted into another world. You had a few Jewish families who lived in this area. We used to call them the "Jews of the Street," which referred to the fact that they must be rich and therefore prestigious. The smell and aroma of kebob and liver on the grill would make us crazy and yet it was off limits; it wasn't kosher. On the pedestrian section there were hand driven carts selling boiled potatoes, roasted corn, and more. Each owner had a special chant of his own, attracting poorer customers and high school students. The theaters were also just off of Chehar Bagh.

Our cinemas had an indoor theater for winter and a roofless one for the summer nights, since it rarely rained during summer. A few years later when I was fourteen, my mother would deprive herself in order to give me some money to see a movie. The back seats of the theater cost the most, then less for the middle section

And finally the least for closest to the screen. I had enough for a seat close to the screen, hiding myself so as not to be seen by the richer Jewish boys in the back section.

My father had a store on the boulevard selling crochet tablecloths and more. It had been my uncle, Joseph, the most avant-garde of the family, who was also very handsome, that had convinced the landlady to rent him this shop. Uncle Joseph and my father would stamp the material given to Muslim women to take home with the necessary threads to do the piece work that would then be sold to customers. I witnessed later how they underpaid these women claiming the women had wasted threads unnecessarily in order to charge more. When I asked why, I was told to keep quiet. Their answer: they steal from us too. Both men would be in depression all year till Nowruz, the Iranian New Year, when tourists from Tehran would come and buy their products. My uncle was drafted soon after to the army and then fled the army by dressing as a woman and escaping to Tehran, the capital.

I remember my mother begging my father during the year to go to Abadan, the southern city known for its oil refinery, to sell his goods. This city was packed with the British who had money to spare. His answer was always the same: "Shut up! You are a woman. You don't know anything!" My father never prospered financially.

Bakeries on the avenue were more than just a sweet shop. They also had a garden where one could sit and enjoy their delights. Among the bakeries there was one called Polonia, or Poland. The owners were man and wife and spoke Polish. Years later it used to boggle my mind as to why these Poles were there. They wouldn't speak much to anyone and spoke very little broken Farsi and always seemed angry. Somehow I am now convinced that they must have been from Yaldei Iran, or children of Iran. This is a Hebrew name for young Eastern European Jewish youth who were saved from Nazis and brought to Esfahan on their way to Palestine. My father used to tell me that when they first arrived and were put in a fenced area, sometimes they would offer sexual favors for a pack of cigarettes. This never surprised me since they had been completely dehumanized by their Nazi captures. Their crime? Being Jewish.

Continuing on the boulevard southward, one would see young veiled prostitutes accompanied by their Madams, nearing the Sio Sepol, or the Thirty-Three Bridges. It is made of thirty-three open arches where water flows through. Each has a built-in large stone table attached to its wall where people can sit, talk, or simply take a prostitute for a quickie. We were told to stay as far away as possible since there were those who would lure young boys there for sex by giving them gifts or even by force. Homosexuality was a taboo and forbidden by Islam, while it had a prevalence behind closed doors as well as in dark alleys.

The bridges were connected by a road that ran above them, all connecting the center of the city to Jolfa, which was the Armenian town.

Eventually we would walk back home in dread of Sunday morning on our way to school. To get to school, we needed to leave the ghetto and pass through Muslim neighborhoods. The older Muslims would rarely bother us as long as we did not walk very close to them during the rainy days. You see, they believed to touch a wet Jew will make them najes; unclean, unholy. It was the young Muslim boys who would fill their mouth with monk lentils and through a thin bamboo cigar-shaped pipe try to hit our frozen ears.

At school, we spent the first half of the day on Jewish studies while the afternoon half was devoted to secular studies. Jewish teachers in the morning, and mostly Muslim ones in the afternoon. School day started at 8 AM and lunch break was from noon to 1 PM, then back to classes till 4 PM. Lunch consisted of bread, butter, and sometimes some jelly, packed by my mother the night before. Each day, a Jewish teacher was in charge of the lunch break to make sure discipline was in place. He would order us to sit on the dusty ground with our legs crossed and have our lunch. He would only allow us to go for a drink of water and back. While we had our cold lunch, the orphans, who had free hot lunch every day, enjoyed their food in the big hall which was otherwise there for social occasions. The smell of the hot food was a killer.

Often, we would save pennies with which we could negotiate a meatball from the orphans. They were not allowed to carry food out of the dining room, yet some were willing to take the risk and hide a meatball in their pocket.

School year started late August and ended mid-June. My first year of elementary school was not a happy one since my mind was not ready to take on all the changes that were happening around me in one year. I flunked that first year of school. I was still just six and a half years old. I remember crying all the way home while other kids pointed a finger at me and laughed at me, suggesting that my parents would surely disown me when I get home. My mother had already made threats in the past to take me to the police if I continued to be a bad boy. I thought now for sure I will be taken to the police since on top of not being a good boy, I had also failed first grade.

As I passed the police station, with my heart pounding, I half closed my eyes and ran, passing the Station like a bat out of hell.

Once home, everyone found out what had happened. They gave me hell the whole summer. From my father to the last, what I got was scorn as they laughed at me. I don't remember how many days I cried till finally I had a sore throat. It was only then that mother softened her heart and consoled me. I promised myself to show them all that I can actually be a good student. I could hardly wait till summer was over and I would go back to school. Once back, I became the top of my class during the entire six years of elementary school.

Life went on as a routine. Going to school, coming home, and doing homework under the light of an oil lamp in the middle of the room. Starting from the fourth grade, my mother provided me with a tutor (an older bright student from our school). Together with another classmate of mine, I would go to his house two evenings a week for his help. Walking through the dark alleys with a small flash light was dreadful. I had learned to mention the name of the All Mighty,
thinking the prayer would prevent any possible attack.

One early evening, while on my way to the tutor, I was surprised when the son of a vegetable seller in the ghetto, who was about seventeen, approached me with a smile, asking me where I was going. Little did I know that the boy and a friend had planned to rape me that night on my way back from the tutor's home.

# Chapter 2

# Out of danger

# Chapter 2

## Out of danger

Half way to my house I heard people quarreling. As I approached them, I recognized Cyrus, a Jewish boy about four years older than me; his house was almost attached to the store of the vegetable seller in the ghetto.

I saw Cyrus and another Jewish boy fighting the vegetable seller's son and his friend.

As I reached them, Cyrus shouted at me: Run as fast as you can, in our Esfahani Jewish dialect. In a split second I knew why the Muslim boy had smiled at me earlier on. I ran as fast as I could while screaming "Help, help," till I got to the door of my house. I kept beating the door knocker screaming "Mama, Mama." Neighbors rushed outside to see what had happened. When Mama opened the door, I kept running at full speed to the most inner part of my home.

The fear was overpowering but I was finally safe at home. I couldn't sleep for nights.

Later, it turned out that, while standing on the roof of his house, which was attached to the vegetable store, Cyrus had overheard the Muslim boy plotting with a friend to assault me. What Cyrus had shouted at me in our dialect was straight out of the bible "and Jacob ran from Esau." That was enough of a cue for me to run. The dialect used by us Esfahani Jews is a combination of Aramaic, Hebrew and old Farsi. We often used biblical phrases metaphorically.

There were other cities where Jews had their own dialect but ours is about 2000 years old and a life saver when we didn't want others to understand what is being said.

As a result of the danger which had passed me, I see enough reason to tell something about homosexuality in Iran of my time. It was practiced to compensate for lack of sexual relations with girls, as well as a tool for embarrassment and revenge.

First, you could not even see a pair of female legs on any lane or street in our city. Girls from age five or so had their heads covered and long pants under their skirts.

Next, they would use veils by the age of nine or ten. Talking to girls was an offensive act and touching them would result in almost a sure death. In an atmosphere as such, homosexuality among boys flourished as one of the two possible releases.

It was also practiced in order to embarrass a person or a family.

One day back from school I found everyone with a sad face till my mother finally told me that one of our Rabbi's sons had been raped by some thugs.

Apparently the boy had a fight with a Muslim and was able to beat up the attacker, which did not sit well with other Muslim boys, which led to the plot that resulted in the rape of the Rabbi's son.

Reza shah, founder of Pahlavi Dynasty, the father of the ousted shah, had tried to prohibit the veil in Iran but had relative success only in Tehran, the capital city. Therefore lack of contact with the female gender was a contributor to homosexuality. Girls simply HAD to remain virgin till marriage.

It was quite customary for the bride's mother to appear at the home of the bridegroom to show bloody cloth as proof of her daughter's virginity the morning after the wedding night.

This was often practiced by Jews as well.

If a bride was proven to be not a virgin, justly or unjustly, her future then was either prostitution or marrying a widower with children 30 to 40 years older than herself.

Prostitution was not encouraged but tolerated. These women would live in a house with a Madam and one usually recognized these houses since there was a plaque on the door saying "No one is allowed to knock the door knocker."

Elementary school years were just routine. I was able to be an outstanding student after I repeated the first year all six years. Nothing special happened till the last year, when I was twelve. Lunch break was a drag since we had to sit down for two hours straight on the ground till afternoon session would start.

Together with my best friend, Jamshid, we decided to bribe the gate keeper several times a week and spend the lunch break outside. After all, the gate keeper was a poor man and could be bribed with pennies.

We left the school for the first time feeling like a pair of adventurers since we didn't know anyone or anything on the outside—our mothers would kill us if they ever found out.

We walked till reached the Shah Square (legend has it that it is the biggest city square in the world, built some seven hundred years ago by the Safavid Dynasty).

There were groups of Muslim boys sitting together on the ground everywhere (I guess we weren't the only two smart alecks in town). Some were eating watermelons while others were telling stories laughing out loud.

I suggested to Jamshid that we speak an impeccable Farsi without a Jewish accent and tell people we are Zartoshti (followers of Zaratostra, who are highly respected by the Muslims—the true Persians following the religion of Sassanid of two thousand five hundred years ago).

Next we went over the three commandments of this great religion, "Say well—Do well—Think well," in case we were tested.

We simply had to fight fear. I suggested we also buy a piece of watermelon and just sit, eat, laugh and enjoy, which we did. We laughed at the loud jokes the other boys were making while admiring the views of two magnificent mosques, palace and the famous bazaar all built seven hundred years ago by King Abbas Safavid.

Horse drawn carriages carried the tourists around the square while fanatical Muslims offered the public free cold water for uttering a blessing to the prophet Mohammad.

On our way back to school we kept on looking at each store. Young boys (as was common) would salute each other by cursing each other's sisters. Very much in line with some Latin American lands where friends greet by calling each other "cabron."

Nearing the school, we saw a group of young boys crowding the entrance of a book store called "Khodaie." Jamshid suggested we cross the street but I said "NO."

"Let's go and see what the commotion is all about." I approached one of the boys.

With a sure face, "What's up?" I asked. He said the book store now has a new policy; you could rent a book for about ten pennies per week. "Wow," I said, "Any book?" He said "Yes any book." Can you imagine? We could take a book home for a week!!!

I knew I must come back and do business with this store although it really catered only to non-Jews.

The feeling I had by the time we reached the school must have been the same as when Christopher Columbus reached the new world.

Having found this book shop, I now had to have a strategy to be able to enjoy its services. The next day I put on a clean shirt, begged my father for a ten rial note assuring him of its return to him by night fall. Together with my friend I went to the book store but he was afraid to enter and waited for me outside.

I went in greeting the owner and asked him to recommend me some books to rent while talking to him with a refined Tehrani accent. He said, "Why don't you try 'Taras Bulba'?" I said, "OK." He was impressed and asked what my father's job was.

I told him he was a businessman with several businesses in different cities.

He asked me for half rial as rent and when I pulled the ten rial note, he said, "Oh don't break the note for half rial, you may pay the rental when you bring the book back."

"No Sir," I said to him and searched my pocket for a half rial and paid him. His smile was a smile of admiration for dealing with such a polite boy!!!!

Carrying the book was like carrying a treasure, thus once home I covered it with wrapping paper not to get it dirty. After reading "Taras Bulba" came "War and Peace" and more till I got hold of the "Old Man and the Sea." This was some book. Half way through, I remember praying at night that the old man will be able to bring the big fish safely ashore. To date I remain grateful to that book shop. The urge to read was killing me.

Through a friend of a second cousin visiting from Tehran, I found out about the "Voice of America" and its publications, to which I sent a letter. Soon after, I started getting magazines about life in America with unbelievable pictures of nature and people.

Pictures of boys and girls in blue jeans, most gorgeous blond girls with their boyfriends in convertible cars, and skyscrapers. It looked like America was on another planet.

I now showed respect whenever I saw American soldiers in their impeccable uniforms, shiny shoes smoking L&M cigarettes while strolling in Chehar Bagh Boulevard.

The dream of America, America was now starting to take shape in my mind.

# Chapter 3

# Bar Mitzvah

# Chapter 3

## Bar Mitzvah

I was approaching the age of thirteen. According to Jewish law, a boy at thirteen is considered an adolescent and therefore responsible for his actions from there on. I studied the part of the Torah I had to read on my birthday while there was no festivity or gifts due to lack of money. Once I red the Torah on that Saturday then women started throwing candies at me
and chanting "Kili lililili."

This chant has a story worthwhile telling. In the bible when Jacob fell in love with Rachel, her father agreed to let him marry her if Jacob worked for him for seven years, which he did. Yet, he gave Jacob his older daughter Leah, who as tradition went, had her face covered on the wedding night thus Jacob simply believed that she was Rachel. By morning Jacob approached his father in law complaining.

The father in law simply explained that he couldn't marry a younger daughter while an older sister was still available.

Jacob agreed to work another seven years for Rachel, which he did and finally married her.

Here then is when a tradition is born practiced and all over the Middle East; on wedding nights women chant "Leah, Leah, Leah" to the bridegroom to caution him about the right bride. With passage of time "Leah, Leah, Leah" became "Kili lililili," a chant of happiness at weddings, child birth and Bar Mitzvahs. This chant was and still is practiced among Jews and non-Jews alike on all festivities. I was now considered a man and thus responsible for my actions.

A few days later, all happiness was gone in our house as well as in all Jewish houses in the ghetto.

When I got home from school on a Thursday, I saw everyone crying.

"Mama what is wrong?" I asked. She said they killed the doctor. "Which doctor?" I asked.

She said "Rabbi mola rabi's son!!!" I screamed "Why?" She said "No one knows."

The Shah had decreed that all medical doctors upon graduation had to devote two years of their time to rural areas helping the poor and isolated farmers before they could start their practice. The only son of the oldest and the most respected rabbi in the ghetto was the first Jewish boy from Esfahan to become a doctor. Upon graduation from Tehran University he became engaged to a beautiful green eyed girl from the "Gabai" family, where my mother came from as well.

The young doctor started his free service for two years and would come to visit his family and fiancé once a month. People became alarmed when he didn't come for a visit for two months and to that end a few volunteers were dispatched to learn of his whereabouts.
Here is what villagers claimed had happened:

The young doctor had taken advantage of a young girl and his mutilated body was the just punishment in their eyes. We never found out whether this was the truth or not.

Another incident which left an impression on me happened one afternoon when my aunt and I left the ghetto to go to the big bazaar; as we reached the street, a bunch of veiled Muslim ladies rushed to my aunt shouting at her "You see Malka has become a Muslim and now has bridegroom, house and money."

They screamed at my aunt: "When are you becoming a Muslim? Don't you want a handsome Husband? Money? Etc.?

30

One of the greatest deeds in Islam is the converting of an infidel to Islam.

Malka was a fourteen year old unattractive, fatherless, Jewish girl. As a poor orphan without a dowry she had virtually no chance of marriage unless to a very old man (as a nurse) or to a widower with many children simply as a servant.

It was at this point that she had been approached by a young Muslim hooligan with all sorts of promises if she would only become a Muslim. Being hungry and a castaway from the community she had realized that there is much chance for her among her own kind and therefore had surrendered herself to this boy.

The morning after her wedding, her husband, Teimur, appeared in the middle of the ghetto with a bloody sheet in his hand screaming at Jews "Look she was a virgin."

Soon after the couple was given a house near ours. Each time my mother and I passed by Malka would laugh at us. I guess it was her revenge since the Jewish community had forgotten about her. My mother took it from her for some time till finally one day she let Malka have it. My mother uttered at her the ugliest insults. It worked. She never bad mouthed us again.

Speaking of impressive incidents, I cannot express the happiness I felt when we first got electricity in our house. It was in 1957.

No longer did I have to do my homework in the light of an oil lamp. What a relief.

As kids we all looked forward to Passover. About a month before Passover, my grandpa together with a few other pious men, would rent a house, clean it and start baking Matzo for the whole community. We were often promised baby Matzos if we behaved and got good grades. This was also the time that boys would get a new suit for the year. Most fathers took an old suit to

One of the Jewish tailors to have it opened to make a suit for their sons. I rebelled this time. Told my father I am willing to go without a suit this year with the promise of one with new material for next year. I remember him getting angry and calling me a gigolo, a gigolo for not settling for a suit made of his old one!!!!! I also made a deal with my mother: I will help my brother with math at the price of a white long sleeve shirt with starched collar and holes in the sleeves for cufflinks. She agreed.

The orphan boys got a suit, which was a gray uniform, compliment of "Alliance Francais."

That summer my parents had to decide on high school for me since the Jewish school was only an elementary one and there were no Jewish high schools. As always, my father wanted to send me to a mediocre one since it was cheap. My mother wouldn't have it, which resulted in a big fight between them.

My mom insisted in sending me to "Adab High School," which was sometimes called "college" since it had been built and used by the British families prior to leaving Iran.

I remember my mother went to her rich uncles and came back with money to pay the tuition and at the same time sent me to Muslim summer school for further preparation and integration into the new chapter in my life.

Sometimes during hot summer days, my mother and I used to go to the countryside watching farmers extracting opium from the poppies. Once the opium was extracted then we took the poppy seeds from the fruit, which had the taste of heaven. Even then I knew that someday I will spend my time in agriculture and planting fruit trees.

Summer school served both as cultural integration as well as a start to get out of the protective cocoon of the Jewish ghetto.

One day at the summer school a boy called me out: "Hey Jude [Jew]: is it true that when you Jews go to the bathroom you use your holy book to clean yourself?"

Suddenly blood rushed to my head and in spite of the fact that I had been foretold by my father never to answer back, I jumped to my feet naming his mama, his sisters followed by the dirtiest words I could find.

Suddenly the boy and his friend jumped me, beating me up but I wouldn't take back my words and fought back till I was on the floor.

Not only they jumped me but they also got the upper hand: they went to the principal saying whatever was needed so that he came out of his office and expelled me, asking me only to come back when I apologize to the attackers.

I reached my father's store with a bloody nose and now it was his turn to punish me.

"How many times I have told you not to answer back to the Muslims?" he shouted at me. My answer was "Why? Why shouldn't I answer back? Why shouldn't I fight back?" I clearly told him that I will not apologize to anyone since it wasn't me who started the fight or the insults.

My father finally went with me to the summer school where I told the principal my side of the story. I joined the class with my head up and before leaving the school suggested to the boy who had insulted the Jews he is welcome to fight me anytime he wants but one to one as men. Summer school was over while my nose was now somewhat crooked for life.

# Chapter 4

# Bicycle Age

Entrance to the main bazar in Esfahan

**Hasht-Behesht Palace**

# Chapter 4

## Bicycle age

It was a necessity to have a bike by the time you were ready for high school since it was the only efficient mode of transportation in the city. Many believed that after Amsterdam no city in Europe or the Middle East had more bikes on the streets than Esfahan. Bicycles had tags like cars and buses and one had to pass a riding test by the city and obtain a license to be able to drive in the city. Once I passed the test with the license in my hand I was now ready to be blessed with a bike.

Together with my Uncle Judah and my father we arrived at the street of bike shops. I wanted an English bicycle while my father wanted to go for a Japanese one, which was much cheaper. It was my uncle who convinced my father to buy me a Philips bicycle. The store keeper suggested I go for a short ride as a test.

WOW! I felt I am driving a Ferrari. I tested the light, the bell and the brakes. It was out of this world. I felt a kind of freedom that eagles must feel when in flight.

For months I would first clean and shine my bike every day when I got home.

I was now registered at Adab High School, had my own bicycle, a few new and clean shirts, two pairs of pants and a fountain pen ready for high school.

I tried to enjoy the rest of that summer by going to Chehar Bagh every night walking this beautiful boulevard from one end to the other while doing my best to go to movies twice a week.

As all other kids, we were mostly interested in cowboy movies while had our fingers crossed that a

French movie would arrive with Brigitte Bardot. She was the most attractive movie star in our eyes.

I also read a great deal while at the same time got a used English text book and started teaching myself English.

Another turning point in my life occurred when I started waking up during the nights with strange unfinished dreams always involved with faceless females.

Some mornings I woke up finding strange spots on my shorts and mattress!!!

At first I thought I might be urinating while asleep and yet was embarrassed to discuss the matter with anyone till one day my mother asked me if I had pictures of sexy women with me. I said "No."

This went on till one day she took me to an old doctor for a checkup of my lungs!!!!???

She first entered the doctor's office alone, coming out minutes later. She suggested I go in alone for the doctor's examination.

As all doctors do first he checked me with his stethoscope, he asked me if I sleep well? I turned red saying "Yes." Next he asked if I woke up during the night. I answered yes again but with my head down. It was at this point when he said: "Listen boy, what is happening to you at night is normal. You are becoming a man."

Of course, he gave no other explanation but added that I should not eat onions, and exercise vigorously before bed time.

His instructions did not help much.

# Chapter 5

# Islam (its appearance in Iran)

# Chapter 5

## Islam (its appearance in Iran)

According to the bible Abraham married Sarah. Sarah had reached old age and, still barren at this point, she asks her husband to marry one of their servants named Hagar.

Hagar produced a son called Ishmael. When Sarah gets to the age of ninety, she is visited by angels who promise her she will get pregnant and will bring forth a male child. Sarah becomes pregnant and Isaac is born. The two boys grow up together till Sarah demands from Abraham to do away with Hagar and her son.

Hagar and Ishmael are sent away in tears, while in the desert an angel appears to Hagar saying, "Don't despair since from your son there will also rise a nation of multitude." Therefore Jews are the seed of Isaac while Arabs and consequently Muslims come from Ishmael.

I always found this event rather unfair regardless of Sarah's motives to encourage Abraham to do away with her son's step brother.

After all, they all could have lived in peace in separate dwellings and thus all this ordeal people go through to date would have not happened. Since I am not an expert on the topic, I must remind myself that there is a reason for everything that happens.

Up to early sixth century Arabs were mostly Bedouin and illiterate while some lived in cities and were more cultured. They were mostly tribes in feud and didn't have major works except providing the Persian soldiers with food and water while others would enroll as mercenaries.

They had no laws or unity. So much so that some tribes would kill a baby girl at birth due to the fear that some day they will be stolen by other tribes. This practice continued till the prophet put an end to it. In short, a people in shambles.

## Mohammad Prophet

"May the blessing of the Lord be upon him" (one is supposed to say this blessing when he mentions the name of the prophet).

He soon became an orphan and was taken care of by his uncle, who was a caravan merchant from the influential tribe of Koreish. He was smart with a thirst for knowledge. Later he worked for another caravan merchant, who soon passed away leaving his wife Khadije behind.

Mohammad, who was twenty-five and much younger than the widow, married her and thus as custom had it inherited the dead merchant's fortune. Legend has it that at night he would sit with other merchants, who were mostly Jewish, around the fire and listen to the words of the Old Testament.

He was forty years old when he was appointed prophet by divine force. His first convert was his wife and the first male convert was his cousin's son Ali, who later becomes Imam Ali. The prophet had thirteen wives and at least one Jewess among them.

He was most in favor of knowledge and hygiene. He made it very clear to all. His decree was that one must believe in Moses, Jesus, but also in him as the last prophet of the Almighty. But he also made it clear in his resale (message to infidels), Convert to Islam (Islam means surrender, referring to Man's surrender to the Almighty).

43

Unlike Judaism, which makes conversion of a non-Jew to Judaism almost impossible, he made it very easy. In fact, anyone who would say the phrase "There is no g-d but Allah and Mohammad is the messenger of G-d" is officially a Muslim.

In Judaism one is supposed to do 613 deeds each day from waking to going back to sleep at night while Mohammad Prophet just issued five:

1. Shahada (declaration: there is no G-d but G-d and Mohammad is prophet of G-d)
2. Five times prayer a day
3. Fasting of Ramadan (30 days)
4. Charity
5. Pilgrimage to Mecca at least once in your life time.

Muslims believe that these commandments were given by the Almighty.

What is most interesting is the fact that Mohammad insisted that he is just a man. He did not allow followers to idolize him. His aim was the recognition of Allah as the only supreme leader of the world.

For the first time (after Judaism) women had certain rights. They were considered as second class citizens but with certain rights. He firmly believed that the rich should help the widow, the orphan and the needy.

People often criticize Muslims for being allowed to have up to four wives and more by contracts. After the Ohud war when many of Mohammad's followers were killed, he saw the great number of widows. It is then that he allowed men to marry up to four women as long as they could support them. It was a wise decision which saved the widows from total misery and prostitution.

In Islam, a man could have a wife by contract, Which is called Sigha. One could marry a woman for one night, one week, one month or for several years. The law might sound funny or ridiculous but it should not. This law was designed to stop prostitution where a lady is with someone else each day. This decree provided the woman with guaranteed food, shelter, and protection.

It is true that the prophet married thirteen women. They were political marriages at best. He remained in love with his wife to the very end. It is interesting to point out that it was Khadija who proposed marriage to the prophet and not vice versa. Once Khadija died, the prophet suffered from depression. So much so that Khalif Abu baker gave his nine year old daughter Aisha to the prophet as a wife (the marriage was not consummated till she reached her twelfth birthday).

To get the prophet out of depression, Aisha tried her best to amuse him. In a joking manner, she would suggest to the prophet to forget the old woman and enjoy Aisha, who is so young and pretty.

Mohammad was a statesman, a diplomat and a prophet. He won over the people of Mecca using psychology and diplomacy. After Mohammad's death in 632 the leadership of Islam went to his close companion Abu Bekr but not all agreed on this appointment. Some actually believed that the succession should go to Ali, who was from Mohammad's family and his first male convert. Therefore the followers of Abu Bekr, who believed religious leaders should be the ones who decide who is the supreme leader, are called Sunnis. And those who followed Ali, who believe the supreme leader must come from Mohammad lineage, are called Shiites.

The two factions finally had a bloody encounter when the two sons of Imam Ali, Hassan and Hussein were murdered during the two days which are Tasua and Ashura about 1350 years ago.

Iran did not become the stronghold of Shia Muslim faith till the 15th century when the Safavid Dynasty adopted it as the official religion. 98% of today's Iranians are Shia Muslim.

Iran became an Islamic republic in 1979 after the emergence of Ayatollah Khomeini.

I had the privilege of seeing the beauty of Islam through my teachers and Muslim friends in high school. They truly acted as brothers and fathers.

# Chapter 6

# High School

# Chapter 6

## High School

There were three of us Jewish boys who had been accepted by Adab High School. We were excited but frightened of what lays ahead. The three of us entered the school on a September day; we were there at 7:30 AM while the school day didn't start until 8 AM.

Wow, it was impressive. The huge open entrance gate suggested having a castle beyond. Once entered, there was this huge road lined with willow trees on both sides. It was so long that you could barely see the many rooms and buildings at its end. On the right side of the entrance road there was a parking place for bicycles followed by basketball court and volleyball courts. Then there was a large garden of English roses which finally ended by physics and chemistry labs. There was a huge square with a pulpit in the middle. On the left side of the entrance road there were two huge Soccer fields.

There was one for the $7^{th}$, $8^{th}$ and $9^{th}$ graders and the other for those in $10^{th}$, 11 and 12 . Soccer was very important to this school since it always won the finals every year; so much so that the red and white school soccer team uniform was the same as that of official city team.

Beyond the pulpit there were two floors of rooms all around in a crescent form. It is noteworthy to mention that the Principal's office located in the middle of the building commanded a view over the whole school.

We parked our bikes and looked in awe. It looked like a million boys were standing at attention on both sides of the road as if the Shah was about to arrive. The three of us looked at each other while my friend

49

Emanuel asked we other two in a hushed voice if we thought it was safe to enter. We stood next to others when suddenly the school loudspeaker was tested. Can you believe it? School had a loudspeaker!! Minutes later compete silence while a paragraph of the Koran was chanted by a devout student over the speaker. This was done every morning while the Principal stood on the pulpit at attention.

We entered a large room on the east side of the building which said "7 grade." It was packed with wooden banks which each accommodated three people. We were about forty-five students in the room.

At this a deputy principal entered while we all jumped to our feet. He ordered each one to introduce himself and mention the name of the school he came from. Now all knew the three Jews in the classroom.

Our first teacher of the day was the religion teacher, who said non-Muslims are excused and may leave the room. My friends and I received some strange looks while leaving the class. The rest of the first day was uneventful but none of the classmates even talked to us, something which did not last long.

It was during the second day when our geometry teacher entered to teach. Everyone knew him in Esfahan. His name was Haj Saied Ahmed Sepehri. He was a devoted Muslim and a Saied at that. (A Saied is a direct descendant of the prophet. They are usually identified by wearing a green button on the chest or wearing a green shawl.) He would teach geometry from books written by himself and also had taught at a Jewish school some years ago. In addition to being a great teacher, he was civilized, fair and a very chic dresser, smoking American cigarettes (a big deal at the time).

Mr. Sepehri approached the three of us and said "So You decided to leave Etehad and come to Adab, hey?"

50

My math teacher was a fanatic. He wouldn't start any session without first mentioning a religious topic. Mr. Riazi went as far as alarming the Muslim boys that they should stay away from infidels when it rains. Why? Because touching a wet infidel would surely make a Muslim dirty and unholy. Many times a session he would ask us to raise our hands if we knew the answer to a given question at hand. I would raise my hand practically each time and always with the correct answer. One day finally he told me to stand up and when I did he said "How sad, how sad. Such a beautiful mind in an unholy body. Why don't you become
Muslim?" I just lowered my head and sat down.

When we entered later that week for the first time in the chemistry lab, we were all in awe. It seemed the British who had the school before had gone to a great deal of expense (thanks to Iran's oil money) to duplicate what they had in England. There was this long counter entirely made of mosaic while every two feet there was a faucet and all necessary test tubes for each student. It was quite a show, the teacher would mix two or three different liquids which suddenly would result in a red or yellow chemical.

My best friend, Jamshid, sitting next to me was so excited that couldn't stop squeezing my hand. The lab made such an impression on him that years later he got a Master degree in polymers from Brooklyn Institute of Technology.

Our Arabic teacher was something else; he would talk to us or rather make fun of the three of us in our ghetto dialect. While the rest of the class laughed we turned red. We had no idea how he knew quite a bit of our dialect. We simply had to put up with him; needless to say that the three of us passed his verbal and written final test with very good grades.

I tried hard to understand why some Muslims behave in this manner with us but could never find an answer. On one hand they called us owner of the book, referring to the "Torah," while at the same time Jews were considered dirty and infidels. I guess every religion has some who are fanatics.

When a week later the teacher of religious studies (a mullah of 30 some years with white turban and black robe) entered the class the class leader got up and said, "Non-Muslims are excused from this class." My two friends left but I stayed in my chair. "Hey, you are excused from this course," suggested the classmates. I said "Yes I know but I am staying." The young mullah wore a smile and said to me "Young man, you are welcome to stay but may leave at any point should you change your mind." I said, "Thank you" and sat down. I figured by learning about their religion, I might find out what makes them different. What made them special?

I enjoyed this teacher and the course. He was fair in his thoughts, out reaching, and from day one made it clear that to be a Muslim one is not automatically granted entrance to heaven. When the bell rang and class was over, he came over to and said "Young man, stay a moment." "Yes Sir," I said. When the room became empty he sat next to me. "Well?" he said, "How did you like the class?" "I enjoyed it," I said. I went on telling him how some of the things he touched upon were the same as in the Torah. "Of course," he said. "My boy, Judaism is the core of Christianity and Islam. We have just modified some laws and added some due to times and changes in human society." I volunteered by telling him that I would like take his course and be graded like any other Muslim classmate. His answer while getting up was most welcome. He then blessed me and said "(Khoda Hafez) may G-d

Protect you" and left the room. I continued taking his Class and passed the exam with flying colors.

What a difference. My only contact with Islam had been with some ignorant fanatics living around the ghetto. Now I was getting to see the real Islam. Here was a mullah (an imam) who treated me like a son. More and more, I could see the tremendous similarity between Judaism and Islam. How sad when ignorance causes division among people.

My contact with Islam and Muslims became stronger once I joined group 11 of the Scouts. As I describe later, I was the first Jewish Boy Scout in Esfahan after the Second World War. Our commander was Reza Navaii, who did not have a prejudiced bone in his body. Soon I had become a second degree scout having eight scouts under my control (six of whom were Muslim boys). We were all true brothers going camping and helping the poor whenever possible. On New Year day (Nowruz) scouts visited the Mayor, the Governor and got invited into friends' homes for sweets and treats.

I never forget the time when we were invited by a successful businessman, Mr. Hejazi, to his house. The servants asked the Jewish scouts to go to a separate room so as not to mix with the Muslim boys. Mr. Navaii got extremely angry, getting all the other scouts to join us in the room set aside for us. Mr. Hejazi had no choice but to apologize.

What happened next was that both my Jewish as well as Muslim classmates became suspicious of me. "Why do you take a class that you don't have to?" I explained to them again and again, "Knowledge is power," but to no avail. Finally, two Muslim boys jumped me, beating me while screaming "Mother fucker, dirty Jew, you shouldn't touch the Koran till you become Muslim." With a bloody nose, I went to

Mr. Berjis (Assistant Principal). He apologized for their actions and promised to reprimand them. I wasn't happy. I thought I had acted like a mama's boy by going to him. I thought what if these boys take humility and civil mannerism as a weakness? Next morning minutes before class started, I threw some dust in the face of the one who had been rougher and jumped him, kicking him everywhere I could. No one moved. They were in a shock. This couldn't be happening! A Jew boy attacking? I left the boy with a broken tooth. Minutes later Mr. Berjis showed up with blood in his eyes. "To my office," he ordered me.

Once in his room, he screamed, "I have had a good number of Jewish boys in this school and they were all nice, polite and good students. Who are you?" he asked. "How do I protect you now against all these Muslim boys? Didn't I tell you I would reprimand your classmates who beat on you? Well, you are on your own now; get out," he shouted, showing me the door with his stretched out hand. I figured I am a dead man. I decided to keep my head up when I went back to class. If I am to die then let me go with honor and pride.

Next morning, when I got into the classroom I was met with nodding of their heads and a smile of respect. How ironic? How funny life may be? They now showed me respect. One classmate even passed on a candy bar.

Next Friday night at the synagogue, I gave thanks to the Almighty for having passed me off this danger. Most of my classmates now were treating me on a one- to-one basis in a normal way and I by turn decided it was time to also have Muslim friends.

Reza was the son of a colonel and once the ice was broken between me and the classmates he asked me if I could help him with math. "Of course," I said. He lived

In one of the best areas of the city full of tall beautiful trees and fancy homes. Twice a week after school, I went to his house to help him. They had a maid who would bring us cookies and hot tea. I was drinking tea and having cookies in a Muslim's home!

It is worthy of mentioning that the Shah took care of the military officers and their families on a very high level. They practically lived for free. Everything was paid for, even their maid. They had free movies every Friday morning at a theater and of course Reza would take me along with his family every Friday morning.

The year ended and most of the classmates passed the year, Reza and I among them as well. Our education system was such that if you failed one course then it was mandatory to repeat the school year, again taking all classes as the year before.

All in all, the first year of high school had been a sobering year, a year of transition from childhood to adolescence. I was blessed with good teachers and somehow didn't want the year to end but it did and summer was on.

# Chapter 7

# Summer

# Chapter 7

## Summer

My father and his partner, Uncle Judah, decided to take
a short trip to Shiraz, not far from Esfahan, in search of a
market for their products.

It was then that my father suggested I took care of their
store while they were gone. I accepted but set my salary at
five tomans (fifty rials). He argued some but finally agreed.

I needed this amount since it was the price of a pair of
cufflinks I had seen in a store window.

Enthusiastically, I opened the store early each
morning and closed by about 9 PM every night.
Ironically, I was selling more than my father and uncle. I
guess I was more charming and people liked to see a
young man trying to work.

Things were going smoothly at the shop till one day
when a major entered and ordered many pieces. I
wrapped the goods accordingly and presented him with the
bill.

"OK," said the major and went on saying that he will
take the goods now and will pay some time later! I told
him how sorry I was not to be able to accommodate him
since I wasn't the owner.

He suddenly banged the table with his fist
screaming: "Why, you dirty little Jew. How dare you talk
to a major in this manner?" I started crying and with an
angry tone told him why he offended me and my religion.
He went on screaming. "I should have you arrested," he
said. I asked him on what charge while

Still crying and angry. I distinctly remember asking him how could a major behave in such a manner?

Then suddenly he threw the wrapped goods at my face and left the store.

My father came back without success but impressed with the amount I had sold while he was away and paid me my salary without arguments.

I took my money running all the way to the store praying that the cufflinks had not been sold.

They were green and beautiful, matching the material I had seen for my new suit. But for now I could only look at them a thousand times and enjoy while waiting for Passover when I would get a white shirt to wear them with.

My father's and uncle's business was deteriorating. At the insistence of my mother, my father decided to take an exploratory trip to Tehran in search of a new place and a new business. He decided to go at the beginning of the summer and take me along as well. Wow, a trip to Tehran? No this can only be a dream.
Tehran? No, this can only be a dream?

Ali Qapu Palace - Esfahan

# Chapter 8

# To Tehran

# Chapter 8

## To Tehran

"Wake up-up, it's five AM, the bus leaves at six AM,"
said my father shaking me gently. I had not fallen asleep
till late due to excitement of the trip the night before. I
jumped up, took my pants from under my thin bed on the
floor. I wanted to make sure they had been ironed with my
body weight all night; yes, they were ironed. I washed my
face, said the Morning Prayer, the "Shema" (hear o Israel
G-d is our creator and he is the only G-d), hurriedly got
dressed and started pulling the suitcases to the door. My
mother handed me our breakfast and lunch and went
together with my father and my uncle, who came to carry
one of the suitcases through the ghetto to the street. My
father stopped a taxi and haggled over the price till finally
an agreement was reached. I just couldn't believe it—
Tehran, taxi, all too good to be true.

Our taxi was a Chevy 1940 which the driver had to
stick a long L shaped handle through the grid while
twisting it rapidly to start the engine. I sat in the front seat.
The streets were totally vacant at this hour except for a
few camel caravans carrying dry wood here and there.

We reached our travel agency, "Mihan Tour Co,"
which was one of the better agencies which did not mind
taking on non-Muslim travelers who looked well- dressed
and educated.

Our bus was a green one from International Motors.
Unlike other agencies that required blessing the Prophet
Mohammad many times before the driver would start

The engine, we all got on, went to our assigned seats and took off.

At 12 noon, we stopped at Qom, half-way to Tehran, for lunch. Qom was and is the holiest city after Mashhad in Iran. There are more mullahs here than anywhere else in Iran. After all, most Muslim theological schools are in this city. It was quite intimidating to the point that my father and I stayed on the bus having our lunch.

We reached Tehran about 4 PM. My first impression: I must be in another country. So many people on the street, tall beautiful three to five story buildings, women walking without a Chador-veil. I could actually see women's legs!! I kept on looking while making sure my father was not aware. Once at the station and off the bus we collected our suitcases and waited on the side to be picked up by my uncle.

I had heard so much about Uncle Josef that I could hardly wait to meet him. Out of the crowd, a most elegant, handsome and well-dressed man approached us with a wide smile; "Oh here is Uncle Josef," my father uttered. He kissed my father then me. "You are a big man," he said. "How old are you?" he asked. "I am thirteen, Amujon (dear uncle)," I said.

We crossed the street while Amujon directed us to a black 1952 Ford. "Get in," he said. "Amujon is this your car?" "Yes it is mine." "Only yours?" I asked. "Yes," he said laughing and squeezing my hand. We got in, in a flash I remembered my Grandma telling me of my uncle's ordeal to get to Tehran. I figured then one needs to be in Tehran to have a car and be rich.

We drove through crowded streets, so many cars but also horse driven carts with a big silo in the back. They sell fresh waters drawn from natural fountains out of the city. Why? "Because water of Tehran is

Contaminated since there is no sewage system," my uncle said.

We finally stopped in front of a three story house with a garden and a garage. I asked, "Where is this place?" "Our house," said my uncle. "All three floors?" He said, "Yes but we have the second floor rented to a nice couple." This was the first time I had met my uncle's wife and children. They spoke with a much refined accent—Tehran accent. When I spoke they found my accent, the Esfahan accent, very amusing and funny.

A few minutes later my aunt (my father's sister) who lived five doors down walked in with her 11 years old daughter Shahin. My aunt kissed me and I hugged her. When Shahin kissed me, my heart stopped. When she smiled, you could see the most beautiful dimples on her cheeks.

What is the magic of this city? Women or girls don't wear veils. People speak with such pretty accents and my heartbeat was not the same after looking at Shahin.

My uncle's house had a large entrance door with an electric door bell. Once in there was this beautiful spiral staircase leading to the second and third floors. Beyond the staircase was the door to the first floor. On the first floor there were seven rooms out of which four had windows opening to the garden. What a view, flowers of many kinds but mostly roses.

In the kitchen there was a gas oven as well as a refrigerator! Who would believe this in Esfahan? The refrigerator could actually make ice cubes. Three story house, car, and refrigerator, it was overwhelming. To make matters worse, I was having this bizarre feeling for Shahin. I would count the minutes till she showed up each time at mid-day. It was hard to take my eyes off her face, her fair skin, beautiful face, dimples when she smiled and her legs. All the while worried if someone realizes how much I look at her.

My uncle took us out several times for ice cream and during the day we all enjoyed his wife's cooking. She was a great cook. Our trip to Tehran took three weeks without any business results for my father. The conclusion was that Uncle Joseph will keep his eyes open for an opportunity and then will inform my father and Uncle Judah to try Tehran again.

The night before our trip back to Esfahan, everyone kissed me goodbye. When Shahin kissed my cheek I felt lightning had struck me. That night in bed I kept my hand on my face where she had given me the kiss.

On the way back to Esfahan, my father and I hardly uttered a word. We were both depressed each for his own reasons. The thought of Shahin was so strong in my mind that the rest of the trip experience became secondary. I couldn't comprehend my feelings about her. I only knew I was looking for her in every corner, street and even my pockets. I kept on putting my hands in my pockets searching not knowing what I am searching for. I had to talk to someone, but to whom? Finally I decided to go to Jamshid's house (my only Jewish friend in the ghetto since childhood). When I told him all about my trip and Shahin, he said "Stupid, you are in love." "In love?" I asked him. He said, "Yeah in love." "Jamshid, is that why I can't stop thinking about her? Is that why her face doesn't go away from my mind for a second?" He laughed. I punched him screaming "Answer me." He said "Yessir you are in love." I begged him to keep it just between us when he dropped a bomb on my head. He said, "Listen: my brother who works at the refinery in Abadan has bought a house in Tehran and is taking my parents and I to live there until he finds a girl to marry.

Incredible, I am in turmoil and my only confidant is leaving me too. I really didn't feel I wanted to live this way. Was Shahin's kissing me a "Bacho del morto" I asked myself. Love is supposed to make one happy. Why then is it making me miserable?

I spent every day of the last weeks of the summer vacation with Jamshid till he left Esfahan. We made a solemn agreement to be brothers forever while promising to write each other every week. To keep my mind busy till the school year would start, I did three things: started reading the "Rubaiat of Omar Khayyam," which is all love poetry, went to pray at the synagogue almost every night, begging the Almighty to keep Shahin well and away from hazard, and got hold of a few silk worms, putting them on elk berry leaves in a shoe box. It was great to see them eating the leaves in a curvature manner. They kept on getting bigger and fatter till they became caterpillars, then, amazingly, with their mouth going side to side, each made a cocoon, all white except one yellow one. I woke up one morning to find the cocoons sealed and no sign of the caterpillars. They had gone inside their cocoons and sealed them from within. A week later each cocoon was opened and a kind of butterfly had emerged. A true case of metamorphosis. Each butterfly dropped some very small size eggs and fell to die. The empty cocoons were sold to a silk weaving shop in the bazaar while the tiny eggs were tied in a handkerchief and taken to the cellar where they would develop into small silk worms on their own by next summer. These diversions helped but not much.

Vang church in Jolfa

# Chapter 9

# Zombie Days

# Chapter 9

## Zombie days

My buddy Jamshid left for Tehran where I had left my heart and I was back at school starting the eighth grade. The year started on the right foot. My classmates were now much friendlier and even invited me to play soccer with them as well as girl watching. The best and most expensive of all girl high school was just three blocks away from our school. These Muslims girls mostly came from affluent homes and although dressed in such a way as not to show any skin except their face, they were beautiful and sexy. The white chiffon kerchief around their head gave them an aura of innocence and purity.

If any of my friends ever got a smile from one of them, it was enough for them to fall in love while at the same time be sexually aroused. As for me, on one hand there would be sexual desires while at the same time great shame and guilt feelings. Why? Because how could I be in love with Shahin and yet have these sexual sensations? After all, I was supposed to keep myself clean and untouched till I marry my love.

When I confessed to two of my new Muslim friends they both said, don't be silly you could love your cousin and have fun too. I became closer and closer to these two friends; Ahmed was a doctor's son while Reza's father was a military man. It got to the point that the three of us sat on the same bank in the classroom. (There were rows of banks each accommodating three pupils.) To everyone's knowledge, teachers included, it was the first time a Jew shared a bank with Muslims.

Ahmed was very funny. He would tell jokes that would give one a stomach ache out of laughter. One day during a class we were told our teacher was sick and asked please to be quiet till the next hour. Ahmed said he had a story to tell us. He started: "I went to my father's office to see him yesterday but his nurse told me the doctor is out and will back in an hour or two. She suggested I wait for my father with a smile. Next she sat in a provocative way and started taking her shirt off suggesting it was too hot in the office." Quite frankly, Reza and I had our tongues hanging out at this point begging to know what happened next. Suddenly Ahmed after a few seconds which seemed like a year said, "I suddenly woke up!!" "You woke up?" we screamed at him, "you mean this was a dream?" "Yes," he said. Reza and I out of anger didn't talk to him for a day.

Months later when again a teacher was absent, Reza asked Ahmed to tell another one of his sex stories, adding "Ahmed I will beat the hell out of you should you wake up at the wrong time from your dream, I will beat the hell out of you. You hear?"

Mr. Daijavad was our new literature teacher. During the first session he said, "Boys I know you all want to know which text book you need to buy for this class." He went on saying "No text book needed." He instructed us to buy a notebook with the maximum number of pages. "Class," he said, "in this notebook I want you to dry flowers, post pictures of your favorite actors, personalities, girls, poems and stories written by yourselves." He continued, "I don't care if they are interesting or boring. We will choose one notebook during each class and evaluate the written part both from the point of view of grammar and of literature. Oh yes, you may air your criticism freely." I thought,

"Wow! What a democratic teacher." What he planted in our minds stays with me to the present day.

Three weeks later I was supposed to present a story in his class. I would both be angry yet tender each time I remembered Shahin, which was most of the time. Angry because she wasn't near and tender when I closed my eyes to see her face with my mind eyes. That was it then I decided, I will write my story about women's eyes.

I wrote how a man could lose himself looking at a woman's eyes being while transferred to a place where there is heaven and hell. Equating the white part of her eyes to a restless ocean, and the pupil to an island perfumed by roses and gardenias. The title of the story was "The Devil's House." Mr. Daijavad was so excited by my story that he had the class applaud in my honor. His course was the main reason why I became interested so much in Persian poetry and literature.

My math teacher and religion teacher were the same ones as last year and was also blessed with my literature and physics teachers, one greater than the other.

During breaks between classes, I sometimes would approach my religion teacher, the vanguard mullah, and have an intelligent conversation on comparative analysis of Judaism and Islam. I must admit that he was well versed in this subject while all I knew about Judaism was from primary school and from grandpa, which had to do now till I got further Jewish education at Yeshiva University later in New York.

Life was becoming unbearable...I started writing poetry while somehow ending each poem with a rose garden where Shahin was the main rose. It didn't help much.

One day passing by the event board I read that a teacher, Mr. Navaii, was inviting new students to become Boy Scouts. The article showed a boy in a cool uniform, beret, and a blue and red kerchief around his neck. It went on talking about weekend campings, helping the poor and sharing festivities such as Nowruz (Persian New Year) with city and military officials.

I went to see Mr. Navaii. "Hello Sir," I said. He said, "Hello." I asked, "Sir is scouting only for Muslim boys?" He laughed and sweetly said, "No, it is for all." "But Sir, Muslim boys don't shake hands with me for the fear of getting dirty." "Nonsense," he said, "scouts are all brothers." I anxiously said, "Sir I am in." Mr. Navaii then said I should present him with a written permission from my father as soon as I could. I left his room elated but also, knowing my father, knew of the tough ordeal ahead. I was right. When I told my father of my decision to become a scout there was simply a No reply. Finally upon my insistence he turned to me
saying: "You are mad."

I asked, "Why?"

"There has not been a Jewish scout in Esfahan since Reza Shah in 1945," he said and went on, saying, "These things are for Muslims not for Jews. You are
going to school to study and nothing else."
I explained to him again and again about the Boy Scouts, its origin and the benefits but he wouldn't have it. I appealed to my mother but he refused her as well. I even had Mr. Navaii write him a letter but still to no avail. I had a fight every night to convince him. It was six months later when my Uncle Yehuda (my father's partner at the store) convinced my father to give permission. I was so happy that I went on kissing everybody's hand at home. I now saw my uncle as a father.

My father called me over and said, "Listen, boy, I agreed with you becoming a scout but am really worried about you since you are behaving like a goy

(Gentile)." It bothered me. I asked him, "Why you say such a thing? What is wrong with learning new things? What if really scouts were like brothers regardless of their religions and creeds?" He answered, "Do you know of any other Jewish Boy Scout?" I said "No." He answered me saying: "Here you have it. You should never trust goys." In my heart, I rejected his comment. Having had his agreement I now had to worry about a uniform and the monthly dues. I didn't dare to bring up this subject since my mother also made it clear that we had no money for this kind of extravagance. But I found a way. I started selling old stamps given to me by a rich cousin while the deal was that I kept 50% of the proceeds. I started selling stamps of Reza Shah (Shah's father), which took me four months before I had enough money to buy the material for a uniform and a black beret. My mother sewed the uniform (it did not look very professional but it had to do for now).

# Chapter 10

# Oil. A blessing or a curse!

# Chapter 10

## Oil. A blessing or a curse!

During the 19th century Iran was caught between the two major powers: expansionist Russia and Britain, which desperately wanted to dominate the Persian Gulf, Red Sea and of course India.

In 1901, Mozafar Al-din Shah of Qajar Dynasty granted a 60 year petroleum search concession to William D'Arcy. Hence the beginning of the problems for Persia (later in 1935 Reza Shah Pahlavi changed the name from Persia to Iran).

The British from the start did nothing but plunder and steal the oil while leaving Iran poor and in misery. They did not honor any of their contracts throughout the decades till the emergence of Dr. Mossadegh in 1951. It was also the British which helped Rea Shah to become the new king (founder of Pahlavi Dynasty) in 1925. Reza Shah also tried to change the oil contracts between Iran and Britain but to no avail.

Finally in 1941, when British forces together with the Red Army invaded Iran to secure petroleum, they deposed the pro-Nazi Reza Shah and enthroned his 22 year old son, Mohammad Reza Pahlavi, as the Shah of Iran. It is interesting to note that the British could not have won World Wars I and II without Iranian oil while they had no concern for the wellbeing of the Iranians whatsoever. Every now and then there would be revolts against the British yet the powerful Britons would put an end to it through bribery and clandestine force.

Who was Dr. Mossadegh?

He was born in 1882. His father was the Finance Minister at the time while his mother was from the

Qajar Dynasty. He lost his father at 10 and was brought up by his mother. He is the first Iranian to receive a doctorate in law in Switzerland. He returned to Iran in June of 1914 at the start of World War I. He became Deputy Secretary of Ministry of Finance and right from the start he combated corruption till 1919 when he chose self-exile in Switzerland in protest over an agreement between Britain and the Iranian government.

As he had predicted life under Reza Shah was tyrannical. For fear of his life he withdrew from politics in 1928 and returned to his village outside of Tehran where he devoted his time to reading, writing, and farming. He also conducted experiments to improve crops and shared his findings with other farmers. Sometime in 1940, Reza Shah had him arrested for no particular reason and jailed him in the north for three years after which time he was returned to his village under house arrest till his death.

Mossadegh envisioned an independent and democratic Iran but he also believed no country could achieve the above without economic independence. He tried to renegotiate and reach a fair restitution after 150 years of exploitation of Iranian oil but the British wouldn't have it. This is when he engineered the nationalization of the Iranian oil.

Once he became the Prime Minister in 1951 he presented a nationalization bill in the Majlis (house of parliament) which won votes of nearly 90% of the representatives.

Once again the British started subversive acts in the oil fields while bribing politicians to act against the oil nationalization. Mossadegh showed how the revenue of Anglo Oil Co. in 1951 was equal to what they had paid to Iran as its share of profits over 50 years. He then went to Washington to meet President Truman. During this period Mossadegh had become the champion of

Abused countries all over. He was so popular that he made the "Time Magazine" cover twice in 7 months.

As Prime Minister and a very popular one he took the role of Defense Minister as well while fighting for a clean government, freedom of religion, corrected the court system, and women's rights. In order to show that he had no interest in joining the Russians, he refused to give an oil concession to the Soviets.

This man was able to balance the budget, increase non-oil productions and created a trade balance all in spite of opposition by the young Shah, generals, clergy, land owners, and the Tudeh party (Communist). What helped him to persevere was the support of the people.

During this period, the British continued inciting division in the land, tightening worldwide embargo on the purchase of Iranian oil, freezing Iranian assets and threatening a naval invasion. The British concluded that Mossadegh must be eliminated. Their efforts worked and finally there was a coup with the help of the CIA and MI6. The Shah escaped to Rome while Mossadegh, who had turned against the Shah, was arrested. The Shah was returned to Iran and started his dictatorial role, which lasted till the next revolution in 1979.

Mossadegh was tried and found guilty—a traitor. At his trail he said: "My sin is the nationalization of Iranian oil and fighting the savage system of "international Colonialism"

He was jailed for three years then under house arrest in his village, he died in 1967 at the age of 85. He nationalized the oil.

I was 8 years old at the time of the coup in 1953, but I remember the events in Esfahan as if it had happened yesterday.

The day the Shah came back to Tehran (with the help of the CIA), the policemen in my city gathered people ordering them to chant "Death to Mossadegh,

Long live the Shah" with their guns in their hands; they would hit someone over the head at random accusing him of not chanting "Long live the Shah."

Further on the road there was a guy who had come up with a genius idea. He had a leaf of paper in his hand with pictures of four lions. He was chanting, "Four lions", you fold the paper this way and that way till it became picture of the Shah. He was selling them at a reasonable price while police would encourage people to buy from him. What was most interesting is what I saw in the middle of Chehar Bagh. A crowd had gathered around a hand driven cart. They had a bust of Mossadegh on the cart with his head covered with a lady's kerchief. They kept on breaking raw eggs on his head while chanting "woman, woman laid an egg." If they only knew what Iran had lost by losing Mossadegh.

The same mullahs who would talk against the Shah from their pulpit now spoke of patriotism and the Shah's greatness—CIA's dollars and employed hooligans had done a great job to have them change their mind. From here on, Iran and the Shah became American puppets.

I cannot help but think of oil in Iran as a double edged sword. On one hand, it should have made Iran a rich country if the super powers wouldn't be so greedy, hand in hand with some Iranians who would only think of their own pockets.

Iran had and still has a great education system. Iranians are ambitious, smart and progressive. I believe we would have achieved much more had it not been for this false promise of oil. Iran is a vast country (1,642,000 square kilometers) possessing many minerals and different climates which is also most suitable for agriculture.

Not only could it be self-sufficient but rather an exporter as well; nevertheless, Iran, together with most other Middle East countries, has become a dumping ground for foreign goods. Goods that Iran could produce on its own with no trouble.

I wondered why human greed is so immense. Why the foreign mighty must plunder and steal from weaker lands? Why don't they understand the fact that they have been blessed by the Almighty with power and as such they have a duty towards the poor and the weak? I guess love thy neighbor as thyself are just nice words…

Oil which was to be a blessing became actually a curse. It made people lazy and with high expectations of wealth. Meanwhile, foreigners paid Iran about US$25.00 per barrel which they would resell to Iran as resulting end products at a cost of US$5,000 or more!

Meanwhile, people held the Shah as the one responsible for their misery. True enough, he was a dictator but this was not entirely his fault. He became tired of being betrayed by those close to him, who were mostly thieves and flies around the sweet. In time, he realized that there aren't many around him whom he could trust. So, he became an American puppet and paranoid about possible attacks for oil by some neighboring country.

While people were dying of hunger, he would pay about US$50,000,000 for each F-4 (Phantom) fighter. In fact, Iran and the US navy were the first ones to receive F-4 fighters. Little he knew what a waste it was. How could he not realize that in case of an attack on Iran, it would be the Americans fighting the war for him not out of love but due to American Interest? Of course, it is also very possible that in time the Shah started suffering of megalomania.

The revolution of 1979 was not caused just because of the Shah. America should share some of the

Responsibility as well. How? Since he would do whatever was dictated to him by the US and being that USA has always been a champion of human rights (regardless of whether Americans practice at home what they preach or not). They should have shown him the way to moderation, respect for religion and democracy.

America had ample time to remind the Shah that Iran is an Islamic country. It was fine and necessary to follow and copy the industrial and scientific progress of the west and not just miniskirts and alcohol. Whether Islam is right or wrong is immaterial. The fact is that an Islamic country should follow the religious laws with some modifications due to time.

At the time of the Shah's reign one could buy alcoholic beverages on most avenues. This angered the majority of people who although not very devout were bothered by this. The USA should also have taught him the benefits of a democratic regime. Not only that none of the above was done but rather he was handed a carte blanche to do as he saw it fit.

When finally President Carter tried to do something, he did it wrong and too fast. Although a devoted student of the bible, he forgot that the Almighty could have taken the Jewish slaves from Egypt to the Promised Land within three months and yet he let it take 40 years. The Lord's intention was first to teach the Jewish people what freedom is and what are the responsibilities tied to it before they reached the land.

One can see the same pattern after the American Civil War when some of the freed slaves went back to work with their prior owners; this happened because they were freed, yes but without proper tools given to them to carry on with their belatedly new life.

As an individual, I firmly believe that President Carter did not do a good job on Iran.

The revolution of 1979 was a necessary step by the Iranians. Frankly speaking, it wasn't all about religion but rather due to immense inequality among the people. It is true that a great percentage of Iranians are not necessarily devout Muslims, yes, Iran is an Islamic country and has the right to practice its religious laws much like other countries. I must remind those who give Iran the "fundamentalist label" that Fundamentalism exists in every religion yet it is never the majority.

Take Israel: again a high percentage of the population is atheist and yet come Friday afternoon Jerusalem is shut down till Saturday night for the respect of Sabbath. Nor may any restaurant in that city show pork products in their windows.

Look at America: many churches of different denominations are in full swing gaining power and followers constantly.

Thus, the revolution in Iran was not just due to lack of respect for the religion but also because of stagnation. The so called "thousand families" lived like lords while the rest had the fight of their lives for their daily bread.

I am personally a witness when on Friday mornings people would line up at Pahlavi Hospital to sell their blood so they can buy food stuff for their families.

The Ayatollah Khomeini was smart enough to know that no one in history had fought religion and won. Therefore, to give the revolution a religious touch was all that was needed in order to bring the people together. So much so that during the revolt days, people put roses in the soldiers' gun barrels and by turn the soldiers would put their arms on the ground.

No one wanted to fight Islam. There was no way the Shah could win a war against religion nor should he have tried it.

The long awaited first scout meeting finally arrived. First we were taught about the founder of the Boy Scouts, Lord Baden Powell, in England and his reasons. Next the leader said, "Boy Scouts are all brothers regardless of religion, race or creed." In my heart, I said to myself, "Oh G-d, I hope it is as he says." The leader went on saying a Boy Scout becomes a third degree scout after learning some material and passing the tests. Then he waits a year and could study to become second degree and finally by passing some other quite difficult courses and passing tests one becomes a first degree scout.

We learned that the main purpose of a scout is to help others while remaining most loyal to king and country. Our leader emphasized we will go camping for a day on Fridays (schools were closed on Fridays— Muslim Sabbath). He encouraged us to bring a friend with us so they can learn about scouts.

After an hour of talking and persuading I was able to have Ahmed and Reza to join me in our first camping. Our group met on a Friday morning at 6 AM in the main city square near the Siocepol Bridge (the 33 bridges in one built by King Aras Safavid some 600 years ago and still in perfect shape and functional to date). Each arrived on his bike with a lunch bag saluting each other with the scout's salute. We moved in a caravan of bikes with the leader first and his assistant riding last. After about two hours we were in the country and stopped near a river close to cultivated lands. Peasants looked us over in our uniforms and greeted us solemnly as if we were the military.

First for about an hour we were taught different knots then some history and finally each was given the task of making up a melodic slogan for our group, which was group number eleven with red and blue kerchief. We were 32 scouts in 4 divisions with 8 in

Each. My division's sign was the eagle. We were to make slogans for our division and for the group as a whole. We laughed so hard at each one's slogan that it almost caused stomach aches.

After lunch, we played soccer and about 4 PM headed back towards the city square where we had met in the morning. Scouts all saluted the leader then most hugged each other to do homework of going to movies together. I thought, "My lord what a conflicting situation." I was the only Jew and yet all scouts treated me as a brother, yet now when I ride back to the ghetto I must make sure that in front of several Muslim owned stores I must get off the bike and pass them with my head down. Why?

Simple, one day early on I was stopped by one of the store keepers telling me, "Hey Jew boy when you get to this point you must get off your bike and walk through with your head down." I asked, "Why?" He said, "It is lack of respect to a Muslim if a Jew boy passes him riding!" I had to obey, specially with the butcher's knife in his hand. But now all in all I was one happy kid. I had become a scout. I belonged to and was accepted by a group who considered me a brother.

Scouting had opened new doors and ideas to me while camping was the order of the day. Camping was the day when we would forget all our troubles in the countryside, devoting ourselves to learning more materials on scouting, planning to help the poor, playing soccer and laughing with no end.

Our leader took us often to visit historical places and mosques which I could never have dared to enter as a Jew. Six months before the New Year (Nowruz) scouts got started planting tulips to be sold through the length of the main boulevard (Chehar Bagh) during the New Year's vacation days. The money earned would be divided between the scouting organization and widows with orphans. Nowruz was special. It was the beginning of spring. Esfahan was packed with tourists from Tehran who would spend the 12-day holiday enjoying our great weather while shopping till they dropped. Esfahan's economy would more or less run wholly due to their visit.

To give you an example, what my father and Uncle Judah sold in their store within these few days was equivalent to or greater than what they sold the rest of the year. On Nowruz first day as scouts we were invited to the state Governor's office, where we shook hands with high personalities, had sweets and each was given a small silver coin by the Governor.

By the end of the first year of scouting I was able to pass the proper test and together with Ahmed and Reza was now second degree scout. A week later I was called upon by the scout leader to form a group and be their leader due to good grades on my tests to become a second degree. He suggested I recruit from the newcomers to the school year. I needed eight boys and didn't know how to approach them or their parents. So what if you are Jewish and need to be a leader of eight Muslim boys? I went on thinking: There is nothing wrong with me, no reason to fear. If I am questioned then my answer will be: well I am more Iranian than you guys since we have been here for 2500 years. Never mixed with Mongols, Tartar, Turks or others.
Therefore who is the real Persian here?

The next day with my head up, I went recruiting, while sure of myself. I explained with honesty what good deeds we do and how much fun we have at the same time. I made sure I got invited to the first recruit's home knowing that if I can impress the first parent then I will enjoy of their word of mouth to other parents.

My plan worked and soon I had Ahmed and Reza as my assistants plus six more boys. We held our first weekly meeting and by vote we named the group Baby Eagle. I chose a blue and white as our kerchief (Israeli flag). Wow I now had to make a group competitive, somehow get the highest scouting honor (which was medal of valor) and make Shahin proud of me, at least in my mind and fantasy since she was so far away in Tehran.

My scouts were happy and soon became famous since we would make up algebraic equations in poetic and verbal form. We presented these equations during our camping with many more scouts and applauded the winner. To get the medal of valor was not easy. It took a lot of preparing, tests and a whole year not knowing whether one would succeeded or not. Among the more interesting tests and tasks there were two:

First I was blindfolded and driven to an unknown countryside early in the morning with a few hard boiled eggs, no water and my scout knife. And of course without company. I was supposed to find water through finding the right plants carrying water inside or rivers, if I found any, and report back to the main square of the city at the foot of the statue of Reza Shah (Shah's father) next to 33 bridge within a certain number of hours. I succeeded.

Second, they assigned me to the task of publishing an international daily newsletter on white cardboard for one school year and displaying it on the bulletin board located on the main wall of the scouts' house in the city. I also had to answer to any challenge made to my chosen topics.

A year later I was officially notified that I had passed the necessary tasks to receive several honors including the medal of valor. I must admit, when I got that congratulatory note, I was proud, happy, aloof and only needed two ivory handled pistols to feel like General Patton.

The day of the ceremonies fell on a Saturday which was a national holiday. It took place at the main square beneath the statue of Reza Shah. The circular area around was packed with people including Jewish parents who would take the family for a stroll in the city on Saturday. The military band played, the state chief of all scouts delivered a short speech. At the end of his speech he asked the Governor and the Mayor to hand out the prizes. I was the only scout who was called up three times to get prizes. Each time I went up, I heard the "Klilili" of Jewish mothers as well as Muslims applauding. I now had a beautiful medal of honor hanging on my chest. I now was respected. I shall never forget that day so long as I live.

Dramatics and theater was more developed at Adab High School than in the others. We had theatrical shows based on Molière's and Victor Hugo's books among others. After each show there would be declamations as well. Here is why I was almost beaten up. There was a religious radio program by a Mr. Rashed every Friday. He had a funny accent and always criticized Muslims for having turned away from Islam. Since I was able to imitate his voice, I decided with the help of Reza and Ahmad to prepare a show and make fun of Mr. Rashed. Finally the night came and students laughed throughout my show and even applauded me. Moments later, my two friends appeared in the back of the stage all shook up urging me to get on my bike and fly away. I asked "Why? What happened? Seems to me people loved it." "We will tell you later," they said, "for now just run!" As my friends and I reached my bike three boys also tried to get on their bike shouting "Here goes the dirty Jew." They went on shouting, "We will show what it means to make fun of Islam." Ahmed and Reza engaged them while I flew away in the dark of night without turning

My light on. While riding at the speed of light I wondered "Why this outburst? The boys loved the show! I made fun of the preacher and not of Islam! Why did they laugh so hard if some found it insulting?" I got home safe. I now knew that Reza and Ahmed are real brothers. I was in their debt. It took a few days and somehow the incident died away.

Every single day I passed by my father's store hoping there is a letter from my friend Jamshid from Tehran. The main purpose of these letters was not just our friendship but also about my Shahin. In my letters to my friend, I would urge him to pass by my cousin's neighborhood and check on her wellbeing for me. Often asked him in my letters to tell me what color of dress she had on when he passed by her house. Did he see the dimples on her face when she smiled? I was mad, mad, madly in love with my cousin, who was two years younger than me, and she didn't even know it. It was not advisable or permissible to utter any words in
regard to my family. Why?

On one hand I was fourteen, which was enough reason for my father to send me to hell and call me a gigolo. On the other hand with the culture we had it would be considered bad mouthing a young girl while killing her future possibilities for finding a good husband.

Among Jews the custom was, first you graduate from a university preferably with a degree in engineering or medicine; short of that you'd better be son of a rich family or a self-made man if you wanted a pretty girl from a good family. Even then, the only way to get a wife was for the young man to be working; a young man would usually see a girl from afar or at the synagogue then have his mother to get in touch with the girl's family. The other way was for cousins to marry

Each other. There was even a short poem saying "Union of cousin is written in the sky."

Each night before falling asleep I prayed for Shahin's health, continuing with open-eye dreams as to how I will build her a rose garden and give her a white convertible Cadillac with wine color interior. My dilemma now was two-fold, first being madly in love with my cousin and at the same time crazy hormones in my body. On one hand I would think of Brigitte Bardot and Elizabeth Taylor, on the other hand, I would scorn myself for betraying Shahin when I had sexual desires.

Often I would tell myself, you should be ashamed of yourself. How could you say you are in love if you have sexual dreams and desires? Are you not supposed to keep yourself clean for your love? At the insistence of my two buddies, I joined them now several early mornings to go girl watching at Behesht Aeen High School located a few blocks behind ours. It was an all girl high school. All the girls were Muslim and from affluent families. Their heads were covered with a long pretty silk black or white kerchief and one could tell their stylish uniforms were made by the best tailors. They looked much prettier than other Muslim girls. I couldn't help but wonder if affluence makes a girl more beautiful. Some arrived by car, some with servants and others alone.

We would be standing on the opposite side of the street enjoying the view while the girls looked on us from the corner of their eyes making believe they don't see us. Oh boy how they loved the attention yet never a reaction except a smile here and there every blue moon. With their faces and bodies in our mind going back to start the school day, it usually took us till mid-day to get our minds out of the gutter.

It was about this time that Dariush, son of a military family who had moved from Tehran to our city, joined

Our class. It was easy to recognize his ability for leadership and he soon became our class monitor (the go-between between students and teachers). He became very friendly with Reza, Ahmed and I. From here on, the four of us would meet Friday mornings in Chehar Bagh and enjoy free movies offered to military families in different theaters. A few months later, Dariush asked me to tutor his sister Mehry in math, which I accepted. Military families were more modern and they would even allow their daughters to talk to boys. They were generally cute and showed more skin, which was in truth a trouble. Look but don't touch. I was warmly accepted by this family to the point that I would ask Dariush's father to arrange for my scouts to get a few tents and other camping equipments from the military

base. He even arranged for my scouts to learn shooting.
All in all 8 grade was a good year both socially and education wise. On the last day of school, the four of us decided to see each other every evening during the summer to walk in Chehar Bagh, see movies and lament for being away from our loves. However, I needed a day job to afford the night pleasures. Through my mother's help I found work at a Jewish jewelry shop where after one week of training, my task was to attach small hanging pieces to silver earrings and necklaces. The pay wasn't great but was sufficient for two movie tickets per week and also covered the cost of broiled potatoes and bread (with a taste out of heaven) sold on the streets. We got together almost every evening walking from one end of the boulevard. In every corner the was a vendor with his cart carrying corn on carbon, broiled potatoes, cotton candy and boiled chickpeas with butter. Each vendor has his own song designed to attract customers.

Since during summer months it rarely rains in Esfahan, each movie theater had a roofless theater only

For the summer. Front rows were very cheap, middle rows cost more while the further rows from the screen (only rich people could afford) were the most expensive. Reason? We firmly believed that being close to the screen could ruin the eyes.

During the second month of the summer I agreed to pick up handmade socks for my father and uncle's store from Armenians in Julfa for a little pay. Hey, don't knock it every penny counted. My father would buy them to resell at the store to tourists and at times to rich families in Esfahan. To get to Julfa first one crossed the Siocepol Bridge (33 bridges) and minutes later you were in Julfa. Julfa was a different world, different society, and very clean and mostly fair skinned people. They were Armenians.

It was by order of Shah Abbas Safavid in 1606 that about 150,000 Armenians were moved from "Nakhichevan" to this part of Esfahan. Armenians continuously were massacred by the Ottoman Empire (those who visit the old city of Jerusalem). They can still see pictures showing towers made of Armenian human heads on the wall of the Armenian quarters.

Shah Abbas had a vested interest in them due to the fact that they were the best in silk trade and artisanship. As such, he ordered their original home state to be destroyed so that they may not try to return. Although the Safavid Dynasty did not have great love for minorities yet Shah Abbas treated the Armenians well. This helped the country's economy substantially since soon Persia had trade and trade roads open to the outside lands due to the Armenian ingenuity.

Jolfa of Esfahan enjoys over 10 churches, public bath, the best pastries, painters, musicians and singers. In fact, the most famous Iranian singer of 1950 to 1980 was an Armenian; his name was Vigen.

The first time I went to Jolfa to run errands for my father, I was in awe. Clean streets (a novelty), beautiful stores, great churches, mouthwatering pastry shops and blond girls. The only thing bothering me was the fact that they ate pork. After all, according to my upbringing, anyone eating pork is unclean and yet these people looked much cleaner than Jews or Muslims. It is amazing how things learnt in childhood stay in one's mind for so many years.

Friday is Muslim Sabbath, Saturday is the Jewish one and for Armenians it is Sunday. They spoke their own language but most knew Farsi as well. Another difference between them and the rest of us was the fact that they used toilet paper while Muslims and Jews always washed themselves with the left hand before leaving the bathroom, never with the right hand since the right hand was to eat with. It took me a few months to get used to toilet paper when I left Iran.

I rode on my bike back from Jolfa very excited and could hardly wait to convince my friends to adopt Jolfa as an additional nightly hang out. Most of the rest of summer evenings we rode to Jolfa and had pastry, looked at painters on the street drawing customers' faces in black and white, we laughed a great deal and of course there was girl watching, but realizing it wasn't love, only lust. Whenever we saw an Armenian with a thick issue of newspaper in his hand one would say to the other, "I bet after reading he uses it as toilet paper," while we all laughed. I guess we were just kids.

# Chapter 11

# A summer to remember

# Chapter 11

## a summer to remember

The rest of the summer went by peacefully. Between scouting events, Julfa, Chehar Bagh, and movies, my friends and I had a real fun time.

The movie which left an impression on me was "Il caso Matei." He was an Italian socialist who fought for nationalization of his country's natural resources.

He had visited the famous Iranian crude oil refinery in Iran, which was the largest of its kind in the world. Matei was finally killed by unknown forces unsympathetic with the cause he believed in. I couldn't help but compare him to his Iranian counterpart Dr. Mosadegh. They were both martyrs.

I was now at school starting the third year of high school. Fortunately, most of our teachers were those of the prior year.

Courses were more difficult and plentiful. We had to take algebra, physics, chemistry, trigonometry, advanced geometry and mechanical drawing.

From early on, my friends and I spent long hours studying at each other's homes after school three nights a week but never in my house.

Our house was in the Jewish ghetto. Jews never encouraged visits by Muslims out of fear. While at the same time, we were poor and embarrassed to encourage visits. This saddened me but luckily my friends were able to understand my situation and never made any remarks in that regard.

We had to excel at school so neither our parents nor our teachers could blame our constant involvement in scout's gathering and events.

One night a week the four of us would ride to Julfa, buying some sweets and pouring our hearts out about our loves.

Dariush was the only one not in love, so he made fun of us and had quite a field day at it until we would punch him a few times.

The climax of the year came a few months into the school year. Iran was to hold the international Scouts Jamboree at mid-summer in Tehran.

On one hand, this was great news and a happy moment while on the other a difficult endeavor due to finances of the trip to Tehran.

Scouts who lived out of Tehran had to pay for their trip. Neither my father had the money to spare nor did I dare to ask him for it. I practically went into a depression. I started day dreaming: imagine seeing scouts from different lands, seeing the Shah and above all prolonging the trip for a week or so to be with my family and love in Tehran.

I simply started praying and hoping for a miracle.

A few weeks later another piece of news: every department may send five scouts to the Jamboree free of charge. Was a miracle about to happen?

Iran is about 1,642,000 square kilometers which is divided into ten departments. Esfahan was the major city of the tenth department, also called "Fars Department"

There were about four hundred scouts in my city and therefore not an easy task to be one of the lucky five to go to Tehran for free.

There was a decision made by the scouts' head master: every scout fourteen years or older may participate in an exam covering geometry, world history and geography. The top five scores will qualify for the free trip to the Jamboree. There was another catch as well. Three winners will be from Esfahan while the other two would be from the rest of the provinces of our department.

The date for the test was set for mid-May while the Jamboree was to take place in a huge park in Tehran in mid-July.

From here on, I walked, I ate and slept those three subjects covered by the exam.

I learned that the best coffee and emeralds are from Colombia, people in Peru and Bolivia would chew coco leaves to keep up with daily life. I even learned about eunuchs In old China (they castrated themselves as a sign of loyalty to their emperors while keeping the cut off testicles in a small box). I memorized formulas and tried to find a name for the geographic shapes of many lands.

One of the most interesting things I learned about in world history was the Magna Carta. Seemed strange that the English Magna Carta written in about eleven hundred was never truly practiced by the western world while the great Persian king Cyrus wrote his version of Magna Carta two thousand five hundred years ago and practiced it so faithfully (no king has ever been so fair and compassionate to Jews as Cyrus. His name remains to be one of the most popular first names given to Jewish boys to date).

Mid-may arrived. I entered the examination hall whispering the name of the Almighty and begging him for success.

The results of the test and the names of the winners were pasted on every school event board about a week later. I was one of the winners from Esfahan. Wow!!!

Miracles do happen. I remember looking up at the skies and praising his name.

The year had been a challenging one but now was coming to a close.

101

Compliments of my English teacher and his passion for teaching, I was now able to defend myself in English but with a thick accent. I read "Gulliver's Travels" as well as reading Hemingway's "A Farewell to Arms." I simply had to strengthen my English to be able to communicate with foreign scouts at the Jamboree.

My interest and progress in the Islamic course had caused a true friendship with my teacher. He was a very progressive "mullah." He encouraged us all in comparative analysis of Judaism, Christianity and Islam.

Every now and then my fellow classmates and I would engage in a passionate conversation regarding these comparisons while cheered on by the teacher. My thoughts were always the same: love thy neighbor as thyself if you are a true Jew, Christian or Muslim. In addition, we had to realize the fact that Jews and Muslims are cousins while Christianity is a branch of the Jewish tree.

I kept on insisting that Islam had taken its essence from Judaism while the prophet Mohammad had implemented and modified many a law due to dealing with certain kind of people and the changing times. He also made it very easy for people to convert to Islam, unlike the Jewish religion. A devout Jew needs to accomplish six hundred and thirteen deeds daily.

In addition, Judaism does not encourage conversions. I always wonder why.

Imagine, there would have been 100 or 200 million Jews. Hitler wouldn't have committed the atrocities he did.

Why then we don't encourage the gentiles to become Jewish? Maybe because we don't want them to suffer? Or is it we really believe we are the chosen?
Chosen for what? For suffering?

102

In the words of "Shalom Aleichem," the Jewish writer: perhaps time has come that the Almighty could relieve us of this honor and simply bestow it on another nation or race.

After all, it is not fair for us to be the only chosen. Let others enjoy this honor as well.

Here is what bothered me about Christianity during those debates:

Jesus was a Jew and a Rabbi at that. He never modified any laws nor did he ever defile the Sabbath or the Jewish holidays. He was accepted as the son. No doubt he was a man full of love but how is it that my brother is appointed the savior and yet they have destroyed me for two thousand years as "Christ killer." Is that the right behavior with the brothers and sisters of a savior?

The above events were the highlights of the school year. Now I had to begin preparation.

# Chapter 12

# A year of anticipation

# Chapter 12

## A year of anticipation

I was back in Esfahan physically while my mind and heart were left in Tehran.

I was desperate waiting for good news of my Uncle Joseph about our moving to Tehran.

I was writing my uncle frequently asking and begging him to find a way to get us to the capital as soon as possible.

My friends and I studied hard. Our only outlets were scouting camping, events, soccer and going to Julfa various times a week.

There were a few events worth mentioning during this school year:

Our department of education had decided to allow young girls of fourteen and up to become girl scouts for the first time in our city. As a result, some of the senior scouts were chosen to teach them all about scouting, which Included relevant courses and camping.

This was the first time I had real contact with Muslim girls aside from my friends' sisters.

We enjoyed each other's company but neither side ever dared to get fresh with the other.

During the Nowruz that year, our group of scouts was invited to have lunch at the house of one of the affluent scouts. He was a good friend and very amicable indeed.

His father was a devout Muslim who owned a transport company and never allowed any of his buses to start a trip without having the passengers bless the prophet several times.

We all arrived at his home on the second day of the new year at mid-day and were warmly welcomed by our friend and his father (women of the house were not supposed to show themselves to us since we were men and not members of the family).

At lunch time, together with another three Jewish scouts who had recently joined in, we were ushered to a separate room from the other scouts. There was a table set with plates and ready.

It was disturbing. Our scout friend was so nice and yet his father would not eat at the same table with infidels!

It was depressing. I suggested we not touch the food and just wait till it is time to leave the house.

It was at that moment the Mr. Navaii (the group leader) entered the room with a happy face and a smile saying: "The other room was too crowded. I prefer to have my lunch here with you guys."

Our hearts were filled with joy. Of course, we knew what he was doing. He was a true scout and a good man not willing to see any of his scouts degraded. We appreciated that very much. By joining us, he proved to be a good scout and true.

In addition, he made sure that the owner of the house said goodbye to each one of us Jewish boys very politely before taking our leave.

By now it had become clear to me that excelling in English and in mathematics is a must if I were interested in a future.

There was a new book store in Chehar Bagh selling mostly Christian books but some novels as well. It was set up to take care of American as well as English customers while residing in Esfahan sent there by churches and companies.

I spent many hours there looking at books and striking up a conversation with customers as often as I could. I knew my English needed much improvement not to mention my accent.

But that didn't stop me from conversing with people. In fact, they appreciated my effort.

The topic was always the same: asking for the names of the best universities, how could a poor student finance himself while studying in America and how could one get a scholarship without being an American?

The answers were similar; a foreign student should have enough money of his own to survive the first year till he becomes acclimated. Most of the Americans suggested I needed at least four to five thousand dollars for the first year while they also told me they knew many foreign students who worked as waiters in the US.

One day while looking at the store, I met a kind Christian missionary. After my usual conversation, he suggested there might be another, alternative, course of action for me to pursue a higher education. "How, how?" I asked.

He said, "Well why not become a Christian?" I asked him how my becoming a Christian helps me with my education.

He went on: "If you accept Jesus as the Lord then my organization could send you to the American University of Beirut for a free education."

It was a tempting idea. I thought how? I am a Jew. I only believe in the unseen Almighty.

I don't eat pork. I can't cross myself. How could I accept that the creator had a mortal son! Even then I believed Jesus to be a messenger and most formidable for introducing love and the power of love. But that was it.

I thanked the man for his offer and kindly refused him.

Another event occurred one day back from school when I found my mother waiting for me with blood in her eyes.

She came at me like a tiger before I was completely off my bike screaming:

"How could you degrade me so much? How could you fall in love with a girl from your father's family? Isn't it enough that this family ruined my life? What do you know about love anyway? You are just a kid. Over my dead body you marry someone from your father's clan. You are a gigolo. Your head should be only in books and nothing else", and finally slapped me.

The secret had leaked from the capital to my city.

I decided this wasn't a good time to argue with her. I simply went inside with my head down and quite embarrassed. Yet, I knew that must have a talk with her later.

I approached her a few days later saying:

"Mom I really love her." She went to pieces again naming my love the ugliest words she could find. She never accepted her and this is when I lost my mother as a friend for many years to come. She kept on degrading me anytime the subject came up until I finally decided to speak to her the least and only when necessary. She had made it clear that from there on I would be on my own.

This was also the year that I became truly familiar with the history of the Holocaust.

I was amazed. What kind of animals were these Nazis? How do you burn six million people in ovens? It was simply beyond belief. I only came to believe when I saw movies of the concentration camps, movies that had been ordered to be made by General Eisenhower when capturing these camps and liberating the Jews.

110

My further belief came when I saw Jewish survivors with serial numbers on their arms.

I wanted to scream. I want to kill every German. I wanted REVENGE.

What was the Jewish crime? Being educated? Cultured? Being patriotic to the countries where they lived?

Wasn't it enough that they were persecuted for two thousand years for being "Christ killers"?

Why couldn't Christendom have learned tolerance from Islamic countries?

I wondered. How much some might hate a race to go as far as mass burning of its followers? Was it because they were considered rich? If so who was guilty for Jews being rich if not the gentiles?

Jews, throughout history, always had to BUY their rights. The same rights others had for free.

So in time, Jews realized that they must always have some wealth at hand in case they are threatened with violence and extreme prejudice.

Such educated and cultured people, thanks to the Torah and to the Jewish mothers who sacrifice their lives to have educated and successful children. A people so cultured and educated could not believe that they will be herded to slaughter houses. They weren't cowardly. They just couldn't conceive that a neighbor could do such atrocities to another neighbor. They weren't cowards. They just couldn't believe it.

The uprising of the Warsaw ghetto is a testimony to the Jewish courage.

I also couldn't help but wonder at Hitler's stupidity. Why didn't he use some of these bright Jews and their scientific knowledge for his wars?

Had Einstein not been intimated by Nazis, he wouldn't have moved to America and therefore would never have written his famous letter to Roosevelt which

Resulted in "The Manhattan Project." In fact, he could have helped the Germans to have the first atomic bomb. I was convinced that hate and degeneracy had blinded Hitler and his hooligan followers.

The more I read about the Holocaust the more convinced I became of two things:

Nations have a tendency to blame Jews for any misfortune in the world, be they wars, economic chaos and who knows maybe even they are held responsible if some wife rejects her husband at night in Timbuktu. In short, Jews constitute the perfect "red herring." The second thing which was becoming very clear to me was the importance of the state of Israel. The state of Israel gave a certain feeling of security and pride to Jews the world over.

Everyone spoke high of Roosevelt and I among them till I found out the truth about him concerning the concentration camps in Europe.

Roosevelt had been told and even shown pictures of Auschwitz. His advisers had suggested to him a bombing of this notorious camp to save the inmates from being burnt.

His answer had been: no let's put all our efforts to finish the war faster and then we can save the Jews. In other words, so what if another million or two are burnt till we finish the war!

The hypocrisy of the western world was amazing. Cuba, America or Canada had not permitted entry to boatfuls of Jews who had been set afloat by the Nazis. As a result, the ship came back to Europe and about a thousand of these Jewish refugees were burnt in the concentration camps. Hitler had shown that no one really cares about Jews.

This strengthened him even more to continue his atrocities against Jews.

Many a night with my eyes wide open in bed I wondered. What is wrong with the Christian world? Don't they realize that their religion, most of their laws and culture are inherited from Judaism? The answer was clear: their hate and jealousy had completely blinded them.

What calmed me down somewhat was my country and its pattern of behavior with the Jewish communities.

We had lived in Iran for two thousand five hundred years. Yes there was anti-Semitism but never in the occidental style. We did not have "pogroms." We weren't burnt in ovens and some Muslims even reprimanded their fellow Muslims when they saw violence against us. They often called us "owner of the book," referring to the Torah.

I thanked Iran in my silence and was proud to be an Iranian. Truth be told, Jews were more Iranian that the Muslims since they remained pure in spite of the attacks by Mongols, Tartars, Turks and Arabs.

I prayed for the day when Jews and Muslims could live as neighboring cousins in peace.

**My parents and uncle with the children together with my maternal grandmother, 1951.**

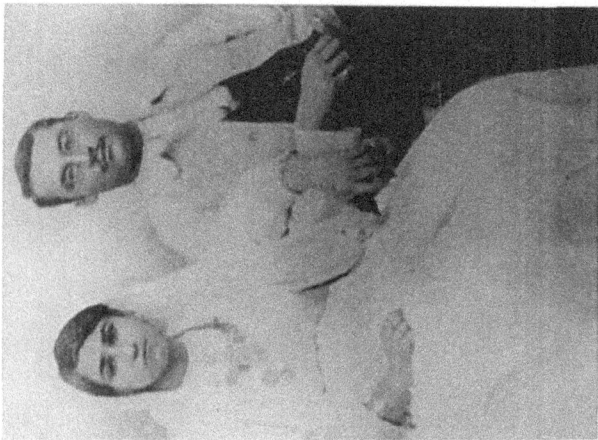

**My maternal grandparents circa 1900**

**My parental grandfather with his father circa 1890**

**A view of the "el Yunke" rainforest from the farm in
Puerto Rico**

**Imam Square in Esfahan where I had my first contact with Muslim boys of my age**

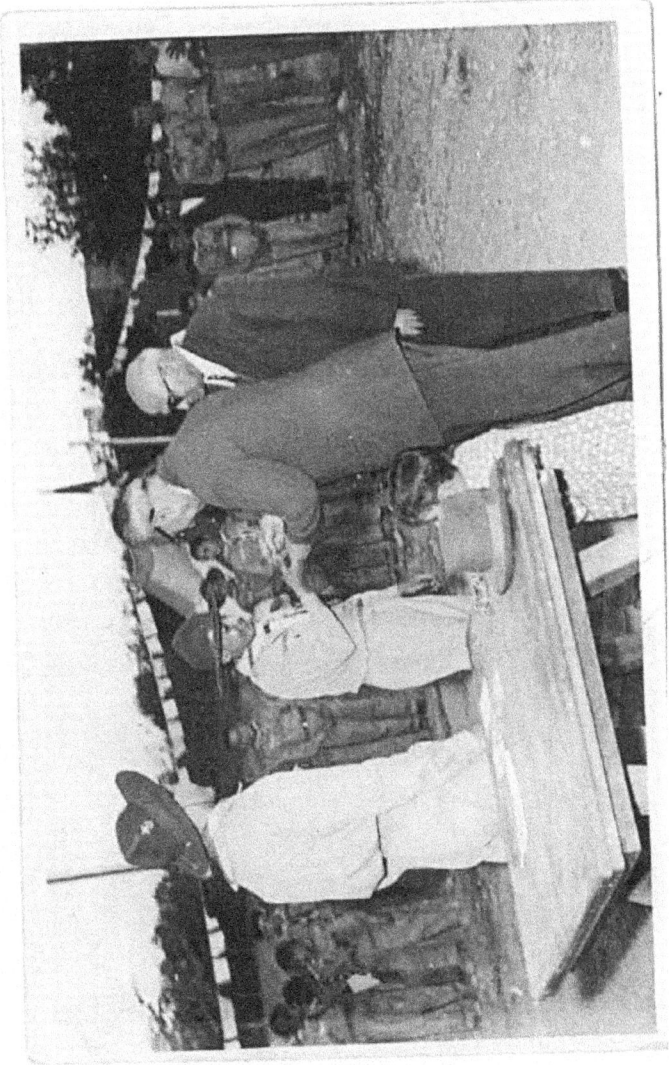

Receiving a prize from the education secretary of
the state of Pars

**My college graduation picture**

# Chapter 13

# Moving to Tehran

# Chapter 13

## Moving to Tehran

The news of our moving to Tehran came near the end of the school year. My Uncle Joseph had fulfilled his promise.

He had found and rented a store in a newly developed part of Tehran inhabited mostly by people from the north of the country. He recommended to my father and to Uncle Judah that they should sell textiles as well as Esfahan's handmade table cloths at the new store. We were to move to the capital by mid-summer in time for the children to prepare themselves for the coming school year.

The most important event of the year was Esfahan's hosting of the national soccer games early summer. Wow! This was like a religious holiday. We now had one dilemma: where to find the money to buy tickets for so many games?

The games started. On the day of the opening ceremonies, I stood behind the fence of the stadium pushing and pulling other watchers to see the game. I had been an early riser to secure a spot near the entrance thus watching the game as well as people entering.

I noticed some young men about my age well dressed entering the gate without a ticket while being afforded a military salute by the gate keeper!

Who are these young men? I thought. They enter without a ticket and are even been greeted warmly. This gave me an idea.

The next day I put on my new suit, for which I had waited two years, my white shirt, green cufflinks and also the scout insignia on my lapel. I really looked cool.

All was well and on my way to the stadium I saw the look of respect in people's eyes. Once out of the ghetto, no one made any nasty remarks or wisecracks about Jews. Some Muslim boys even saluted me!

I was encouraged by this behavior of people and hoped my idea would work.

I finally reached the stadium and went in through the gate with a snobbish smile at the gate keeper.

"Excuse me," said the gate keeper.

I politely answered with a firm "Yes?" He went on: "Aren't you the son of such and such General?" I nodded my head smiling.

At this point, he gave a military salute and ushered me into the stadium. I politely thanked him and went on choosing one of the best seats in the front row.

Wow! My idea had worked. It had worked since most people judge by their eyes.

I now had free access to all games and at times even took Reza and Ahmed with me, of course for free as well. To make sure the gate keeper was kept happy, once in a while I put a five rials coin in his hand for which he was most grateful.

The games ended with the usual results: Tehran in the first place and Esfahan in the second.

The rest of the remaining time in Esfahan was spent packing, buying gifts for the relatives in Tehran and saying goodbyes to family and friends. My friends and I spent every moment available going to Jolfa and to the movies.

It was a time to rejoice but also a sad moment for me. I now had to leave my friends who had become like brothers. We agreed not to say goodbye while promising each other to write letters at least once a

Month. This promise was honored till I left the country a few years later.

It was truly hard to leave Esfahan due to all the memories and great friends while at the same time it was a great changing moment in my life. I was going to the city of opportunities and the city where my love lived. Somehow Tehran looked nearer to America than Esfahan did.

Finally my father and uncle, who had gone ahead to find suitable apartments, gave us the green light. All packed we got on the bus on our way to a new city and to a, hopefully, better life.

Little I knew about the problems, embarrassments and discomforts which lay ahead.

# Chapter 14

# Life in Tehran

# Chapter 14

## Life in Tehran

We arrived in Tehran tired and packed with suitcases and boxes.

We were herded to a second floor apartment consisting of a large L shape room with no separating wall or even a kitchen.

My mother went wild. "Where do I cook?" she asked angrily. The landlord uncaringly suggested she use the outside linen closet as a kitchen.

I remember her sitting in a corner crying and blaming her luck as a woman.

I was equally upset at what I saw. We had left a big house of many rooms, large garden with pomegranate trees for this? I realized no one will have any privacy in this apartment.

When I asked my father "Why such a small apartment?" he told me how very expensive rental apartments were in the capital.

Without any further complaints, I took one of the extreme corners of the room, a space about five square feet, as my new room, arranging my books as a headboard while my bed consisted of a sheet on the floor, a pillow and a blanket. This was to be my room where I did my homework and slept till I left Iran.

I was awakened early next morning by my father telling me to find a cheap high school.

High schools in Iran were all private and very much a lucrative business. Often a few teachers got together and rented a residential home forming a high school consisting of a few rooms, small yard and virtually no laboratories of any kind.

Tehran had two magnificent high schools, one was called "Alborz" and the other "Hadaf."

They looked like university campuses with all the necessities that a student may need.

These two schools were not accessible just to any boy. To be able to enroll at one, a boy needed to be a very good student indeed as well as very rich to afford the tuition. There was no such thing as scholarship.

I got on my bike and went straight to my friend Jamshid's house. I figured it would be great if I enrolled at the same school he was studying. This way, I wouldn't miss my friends in Esfahan so much and at the same time have someone who could teach me more about this new city.

He took me to his school, which, as I thought, was a residential house of six rooms converted into a high school.

I said to Jamshid: "How can this be a school?"

He laughingly said: "Forget about your 'Adab High School.' This is Tehran and we are lucky to study at this place since teachers are not bad and the tuition is affordable."

Schools as such did not care whether a student had high credentials or not. It was like a factory.

He introduced me to the Assistant Principal. The man smiled when he saw me coming from Adab but wanted to know how rich my father was. I explained to him how my family had come to Tehran in search of a better life. He decided I will pay the same as Jamshid. Although he had been reasonable, the tuition was at least four times greater than tuition fees asked by any high school in Esfahan.

My father agreed to pay the tuition fee with one condition: I had to find a summer job later to pay the next year's tuition and the year beyond on my own. I had no other choice but to agree with him.

The first day of school was surely a strange one. Over two hundred students were packed in one hundred or so square feet in the yard. We were finally assigned to a room and each room had about forty students.

Most of the boys spoke Turkish as well as Farsi. They were from the north of Iran whose parents had migrated to Tehran and almost all of them were involved in construction.

They were a rough bunch and most of them were built like bulldozers.

They didn't care much for learning. Their priorities were their hair style as well as cutting classes to go to movies. There was no discipline of any kind. They walked in and out of class at their pleasure and gave a hard time to teachers.

The only time we could learn something was during the math and science classes since these subjects were taught by the Assistant Principal whom they respected somewhat.

Students in Tehran had many strange behaviors among which I found one most bizarre:

If a student wanted to talk to the teachers or answer a question, he would refer to himself as "We"! Like: "Sir, we know the answer" or "Sir, can we talk?"!

I kept on asking myself, why does he refer to himself as "we"? Why doesn't he say "I"?! According to Jamshid this had to do with extreme self-confidence, arrogance and vanity. I never got used to it nor did I ever copy this behavior.

I felt we weren't learning as much as we should in math and sciences. To find out about our school standards of teaching, I got hold of a used math text book used by one of the two elite high schools. I was overwhelmed. I couldn't believe the poor standards of my class.

When I showed the book to my math teacher, he paged the book, smiled and thanked me for being such a serious student. He further asked me if he could borrow it for a while. I gladly said "Of course."

He entered the class during our next math session with blood in his eyes.

He asked me to stand up and went on saying to the class: "Once in a while a teacher is blessed with a student who wants to learn," pointing at me, "in spite of some of his classmates who feel they come to school as a pastime."

He became demanding from there on using the text book I had lent him to teach us on much higher level.

This prompted most of my classmates to dislike me. They started cursing me in Turkish and for the first time in Tehran I now heard ugly comments about Jews. Although a few students were on my side it did not pacify those who now hated me for wanting to learn.

To make matters worse was the atmosphere in our apartment.

My father wasn't doing well which was enough to shatter whatever was left of my mother's dream of a better life in Tehran. She was always in a bad mood and prompting fights with anyone around and with me in particular.

She had adopted my feelings about Shahin as scandal and had her and I as her scapegoats. She called her ugly names while my title had become "the gigolo." I fought her back till I gave up. From there on, I would get on my bike and go to the airport whenever I saw a fight was coming.

I watched planes arriving while others left. It gave me a sense of freedom. I looked at he colorful plane lights and dreamed of the day I will be free.

My only other source of relief and entertainment was going to my uncle's house on Fridays, watching

Television and eating delicious foods prepared by his Wife.

My uncle consoled me constantly and reminded me that better days for me lay ahead.

Summer started and thanks to my uncle who helped me find a job at textile store in the downtown area now had the summer cut out for me.

I went to work daily except on Sabbath from ten in the morning till seven in the evening.

My lunch consisted of a sandwich of bread and butter almost always.

One morning before going to work, I went to the Iran-America Society to find out about their English classes.

I was told there were eight grades to be completed to finish the school and anyone trying to enter first had to take a test to establish his knowledge of English first.

I took the test and went back for the result a week later. A secretary informed me that the Principal wished to see me. She ushered me to his room. I politely said "Good morning, Sir." He answered the same and offered me a seat.

"When and where did you study English?" he asked. "Just in high school and on my own, Sir," I volunteered.

"Did you cheat on the test?" he asked. I firmly said "Of course not, Sir."

Amazingly he added: "No one of your age has taken this test and been qualified to enter our sixth grade"!

He shook my hand and told me I would be welcome in once I paid the tuition fee.

I left the place happy but wondering when I could bring two hundred rials to pay the school. I couldn't touch the money earned for the summer job since that had to pay for the next school year. What do I do?
Where do I go?

As always, I had one chance. Ask my uncle. What if he gets tired of doing me so many favors? But I had no one else to go to.

His business wasn't as good as before. Nevertheless, he asked me to give him a week or two to provide me with the tuition fee.

He gave me the money a month later. I started attending the English classes two nights a week from seven thirty in the evening till nine at night.

Our teacher was a young American diplomat who taught English as a side job.

He was kind with typical American clothing as we often saw in the movies.

He smoked Pall Mall cigarettes in a very cool manner and threw away his cigarettes butts while they were still worth smoking five or six puffs. I thought he must be rich.

I practically swallowed every word he taught us and soon became good friends to the point that he often offered me a cigarette when he smoked one himself.

I bombarded him with questions about America after each session while he answered each patiently and kindly. He gave me hope about the future. He was a nice fellow indeed.

I took another test four months later and was upgraded to the final, eighth, grade.

My problem was again the tuition. There was no way that I could approach my uncle again. I had to tell my teacher how unfortunate it is that I won't be able to finish the course due to my financial problems. He urged me to talk to the Principal and promised me that he would talk to him on my behalf as well.

When I saw the Principal he said: "It would be a shame for you to stop. You may continue your last class for free." He added: "You deserve it." I did not know how to thank him or my teacher.

132

Both summer vacation and summer job had ended. I paid for the year's tuition from my earnings and went on with the school year.

Our teachers were the same except the English one. He was a Tank Corp. Major.

Major Ahanchi was an American-educated Iranian who had excelled in wrestling, which had helped him to get to high places. (It was well-known that Iran had a very strong Olympic wrestling team which collected most of the gold medals offered in this sport during the Olympics from the 1950s to the late 1960s.)

Major Ahanchi was the head of the wrestling federation with his office in one of the newest and tallest high rises built by the Shah to promote this sport. The purpose was to make Iran famous and known to the world. The Major taught English on the side just to kill some time and to continue to practice his English as much as possible.

He took an immediate liking to me when he realized my English was well ahead of my classmates. He liked hard working students since he himself had come from a poor family. He even gave me a gift when I passed my final exam at the Iran-America Society.

He proudly showed my proficiency certificate to famous wrestlers and friends.

Soon he became busy with Olympic preparations and asked me for my help. He asked me to fill his place as the English teacher, with the permission of the principal, for a few weeks and further asked me to prepare the final test, which I was to present to him for his approval before it was given to the class.

As the saying goes, every dog has his day. I now had mine. I now held my ground especially with the same Turkish boys who had offended me so many times. But when they came for a truce, I was open. I was open since I knew the best arrangement would be a

Peaceful one. They now respected me and even offered me pictures of naked woman if I wanted any. We were now good friends.

The day I took the test to the wrestling federation building was quite a day. What a magnificent building it was. Offices were spacious and well furnished with all amenities one could ask for.

I went straight to the Major's office, which was the best room of all. He took me by the hand saying "Come I want you to meet some people." When we entered a large room, my mouth was left wide open! Wow. All the gold medalists were there. These were men that one only saw on television and yet I was seeing them in real life and even shook their hands.

They gladly agreed to take a picture with me while offering me the most decadent sweets and cold drinks.

The Major approved the final test. I left that building feeling important and happy.

I now had both my uncle and the Major as my mentors.

Soon the Major had accepted an additional function as the President of the Tank Corp. Resort Club. It was a club with swimming pool, shooting gallery and theater with a vast park suitable for picnics.

He approached and gave me a membership card to this club one day after class and said, "Thank you for your help with the class while I was busy with Olympic Affairs."

It was hard to believe that at seventeen I had a membership to an elite club while my family and I lived in a one bedroom apartment.

I thanked him very much but reminded him that my being a Jew might cause trouble at the club.

"Rubbish," he said. "Just tell them you are my nephew if anyone ever asks."

He suggested I pay a visit to the club and enjoy the amenities offered while he made sure to tell me to enjoy the girls in their swimwear.

But I was still scared and found it daring. What if they found out I am a Jew?

He assured me there was no need to be scared and wished me a good time.

Once again I was the only Jew and a very young man at that to become a member of an establishment as such.

I enjoyed the club as often as possible where I made many friends. It was a place of fantasy. I felt important and equal to the rest for a few hours. I saw how beautiful people lived and hoped for the day when I would be successful and comfortable.

It is a custom in Iran to visit friends and relatives during Nowruz (the New Year).

I bought some flowers and went to visit the Major and his family. He was delighted to receive me and after introducing me to his wife and to close family members took me on a tour of his beautiful home.

The Shah went out of his way to show kindness to the military for their support and to Olympic athletes with the hope of making his country famous. I had no doubt that he had received help to buy a house this pretty.

The walls of their living room in the house were covered with medals and their written orders by the Shah. It was truly impressive. There was a large table covered with typical New Year sweets from one end to another. After drinking tea with mint and devouring some sweets, he called me over and pointed out at a pretty girl of about fourteen saying "She is my niece, Yigal. I would love to see you marrying her." I laughed and said, "But Major, you know I am in love with my

135

Cousin. Who knows better than you about this love and my sufferings?"

I had several times spoken to him about Shahin and each time he had told me to be patient.

I continued: "Major, remember I am Jewish while your niece is a Muslim."

He laughed. "My boy, you marry them both. First your cousin and then you will convert and marry my niece." Somehow he made sound very easy.

Before I left his house, he suggested I finish high school first then he would send me to West Germany to study naval engineering. He made it clear that by pulling some strings, I could accomplish the task for free as long as I would come back and join the military.

It was a tempting offer: studying engineering for free and also marrying his pretty niece.

I hugged and thanked him telling him how grateful I was but my mind was set on America.

By now my mother and I rarely talked to each other. I had to defend my cousin's good name each time she insulted her in her absence.

One day, she suggested I accompany her to the home of her well-to-do cousins Ester and Masuda. They were daughters of her aunt with their own children of my age and younger.

Both sisters with their families lived in a huge three story house in a most affluent part of the city. Their husbands had a Persian rugs and antiques gallery. Most of their clients were Americans and Europeans.

It was confusing to see which child belongs to which sister since each of the two ladies acted as the mother of all their nine children. I was accepted with open arms and almost from the start was treated like the other children by the two women.

My mother's astuteness had worked. She had been able to get me away from my father's family and lured

Me to hers. I didn't mind since I found genuine kindness in these new relatives right away.

To be honest, I wasn't much surprised at their generosity and their open door.

Their father, Monsieur Shalom, was a self-made man and an expert in the French language. Having come from a poor family and an orphan from early age he knew what it was like to be poor. As a result, he had become a famous philanthropist who helped indiscriminately. If a poor person approached him, he never asked about his religion or belief. He simply asked what the man or the woman needed. That was all.

Having heard of my progress in English and math, the two sisters asked me to be a tutor to their children which I gladly accepted. I went to their house three nights a week. First was the tutoring and then listening to rock songs on their record player till late at night.

I ate there, slept there and had truly become like another son to the household.

The two sisters and their mother, my mother's aunt, showered me with gifts consisting of American shirts and other things bought from their American clients.

There was flirting with new female cousins and brotherhood and friendship with the male ones of my age.

All this had helped my relation with my mother to improve. We started having short conversations where the subject was always the same: how my father had shattered all her dreams and hopes about a good life where her children would have lived in utmost comfort. I by turn kept on telling her not to worry since I will become successful and will help her to materialize some of her dreams.

I was becoming content with my lot. I loved my cousin and had two mentors. Also thanks to my newly found cousins I now enjoyed a better life and found

Many new friends from affluent Jewish families who were close to these relatives.

At the beginning of the last year of school, my parents kind of made it clear to me that I will be on my own once done with high school. This prompted me to initiate my plans and efforts for going to America just as soon as the year ended.

To get a student visa for America I first needed to receive an I-20 form from an accredited school. This form was granted to a student with high school good grades and with strong finances guaranteeing the student's wellbeing while in America. The latter part was done by showing bank accounts and proof of wealth through business or land ownership.

I had good grades but that was all. I searched and searched for a solution with no result.

There was simply no alternative course of action at hand. The year was coming to an end while my top priority was my getting to the USA.

I spoke to my uncle. No solution. I drove the Major crazy with my questions and my dilemma. His answer was the same: "I am thinking, I am thinking."

The Major finally had an idea:

He said, "The main problem is how to get to America, right?" I said, "Right."

He suggested I somehow try to get a visitor visa. We both knew this would impossible since the American consulate knew that young people without an I-20 form asking for tourist visas simply want to get away. They did not need parasites nor extra load on their shoulders in the USA.

The Major ordered me to start thinking and coming up with a plan. He thought I was smart enough to find a way to get a visitor visa.

He also made it clear that knowing me, I won't die of hunger. He suggested, once in America I will easily find a job as busboy or a waiter to sustain myself.

Before letting me go, he highly recommended that I stop thinking of Shahin so much and get down to the business of America.

The Major was right. I had two problems and needed to solve one at a time.

I saw my cousin and asked her for the last time if she loved me. No answer.

That did it. I decided to keep a low profile but still very much in love.

I stayed up in my corner night after night thinking about a visa but found no way to get one.

It was during one of these white nights that I decided to come up with a hypothetical solution much like solving a three dimensional geometry problem.

I asked myself: why and when would I grant a tourist visa to a young man if I were a US consul?

I figured I would issue him a visa if I found him to be well educated, pleasant, spoke English and rich. As a consul, I would be led to believe that the man is going for vacation.

That was it.

Suddenly I had come up with a great idea.

# Chapter 15

# Trying to get an
# American tourist visa

# Chapter 15

## Trying to get an American tourist visa

My plan was to make myself pass as a well-educated rich high school student when going to the US consulate to get a visa. The reason for my trip would be to spend part of the summer vacation with a cousin, once removed, who was studying at California Polytechnic Institute in California.

Next I had to establish myself to be from a rich family. How? Knowing how people judge by their eyes, I needed to appear at the consulate very well dressed and groomed from head to toe.

Next I practiced imaginary conversations with the consul over and over again polishing my thick accent all I could.

I went to my newly found rich cousins to borrow a nice suit, a shirt and a tie.

They owned a gallery packed with antique Persian rugs as well as other rare Persian antiques on the most famous commercial avenue in the city. Most of their clientele were Americans who often invited my cousins and their parents over to their houses.

My cousins received many gifts, including clothing and others from them during almost each of their visits. My suit to wear for the consulate had to be from these gifts.

I borrowed a nice light blue suit, made in America, a white shirt and a red tie.

Next I went to my uncle who used to wear the most expensive shoes made by the most well-known shoe shop in Tehran. By looking at the shoes one knew they came from that shop.

He lent me a beautiful pair which I adjusted the size of by putting some cotton balls in the toes area. Also I borrowed from the Major his impressive watch the day I was going to the consulate.

One early morning, I got up, shaved, put on my clothing, said a silent prayer and off to the consulate hopefully to get a visa.

I joined a long line of people waiting to be attended. We each were given a form which needed to be filled out and handed to the clerk while waiting for our names to be called.

I made sure the address I wrote on the form as mine was that of my uncle due to the affluence of the area where he lived.

After about two hours, which felt like an eternity, my name was called out and I was ushered to one of the consuls' offices.

Upon my entrance I wished the man "Good morning, Sir." The consul nodded his head. Next he picked up his phone and asked for a translator. I thought here was a chance for a good start.

I jumped from my seat. "No, Sir we won't need a translator. I do speak English," I claimed.

He had a wide smile of satisfaction on his face. "How nice. I am glad," he said while kindly motioning me to sit down.

"Where did you learn English?" he wanted to know. I told him how I owed my limited knowledge of this language to high school, to the Iran-America Society as well as to writers like Hemingway. He now seemed even more pleased. The more we talked, mostly about writers, the more impressed he showed to be.

Then he changed the subject suddenly.

"Where would you stay while in America?" I told him "With my cousin." Would I want to study in America? Here I had to be careful with my answer.

My reply was: "Sir, I might but for now I need to study near the family since I might be required to give a hand with our family held businesses."

At this, he started writing notes for a minute or two in absolute silence.

I thought to myself: what if he asks me about my family business? What if he has realized what I am doing? He finally broke the silence and got off his chair, walking towards me.

He said: "It has been a pleasure to meet such a bright young man. Have a safe trip to California," while he shook my hand repeatedly. It couldn't be. It is impossible. He couldn't have given me a tourist visa so easily. But in fact he had.

A clerk gave me back my passport with the prettiest colorful seal on one of the middle pages which said Tourist Visa.

I was no longer walking on the ground but rather on the clouds. How could it be? I thought Americans seem to believe people since they themselves never lie and thus feel everyone is like them? Or was it that the consul truly believed me to be a young boy with a bright future?

No one absolutely no one among the relatives and friends could believe that I had received a tourist visa. It was simply unheard of. Both the Major and my uncle couldn't hide their amazement.

I got started. First, I had my high school records officially translated. Next I took a one month accelerated course in typing since my cousin studying in California had made it clear in his letters the importance of typing when it got to the writing of term papers in college.

I kept on looking at my visa, constantly thinking of how I will pay for my plane ticket which was a small fortune. To escape from the reality, I tutored, went to

The military club or spent time in my cousins' house. I had to come up with some solution. Plane ticket and some initial money for when I get to the US were hard realities.

In a garden party at the Iran-America Society I became very friendly with an American diplomat whom I decided to confide in.

I told him everything about my situation and the getting of my visa in spite of the fact that I had not enough money to exist for a while in the US while I found a job.

First came his amazement and then his genuine concern about my wellbeing in America under the current circumstances. He was strongly against me leaving Iran without sufficient money to sustain myself at least for a year let alone the college tuition.

He tried his best to change my mind but without success.

It was two days later when my uncle gave me the dreadful message. The American consulate had called my uncle's home leaving the following message: I was supposed to go back to the consulate immediately regarding an urgent matter having to do with my visa. I thought of the worst. I figured the consulate knows the truth. I wasn't wrong.

I dragged myself to the consulate shaking. I was asked for my passport which I reluctantly handed in.

Minutes later appeared the same good consul who had issued me the visa with my passport in his hand.

He handed me back my passport and simply said how sorry he was with a grim face.

Hastily I opened my passport where I saw the word CANCELED stamped on my visa three times. Life was over. I was dead.

I really don't know which made feel worse. Looking at the consul or thinking of my canceled visa.

I only knew one thing for certain. There was no reason to live for. How did they find out? I kept asking myself. Was it the diplomat who warned them? It didn't matter now. All was lost.

Depression took over. I didn't want to get out of my bed. I turned against the world.

Why some have all the luck and money in the world while others are simply hand and mouth? At one point, I came to the conclusion that Communism must be the answer. I was angry. I wanted to scream. I wanted to cry. I simply wanted the world to stop so I could get off. At the same time, I knew that I and only I was responsible for my defeat and no one else.

When the news got to Benjamin, my youngest uncle from my father's side in Israel, who was an instructor at a university, he suggested I try Israel. In his letter he wrote how people all live almost alike and how rich is not a "master" in Israel? He agreed that in America it would be easier to progress financially but that Israel held the promise of the future.

To the best of my recollection, Iranian Jews thought of immigrating to the Promised Land when they faced severe economical problems or family scandals. It is true that there were also young Jewish Zionists who believed in going to Israel or bust. My Uncle Benjamin had been one of them.

I wasn't a Zionist but firmly believed in the importance of Israel on two levels:

There had to be a Jewish state so NO one could burn my brothers and sisters in the ovens again.

The second reason for its importance was the fact that Jews could walk straight and with their heads up the world over as long as they had a country of their own.

America had been on my mind all my life but now I had to consider the possibility of going to Israel instead. Another added benefit was having my Granma and two aunts who lived in Israel as well. They would surely take good care of me I figured.

There wasn't much more I could do when my parents approached me saying. "This is it; we can no longer afford having you here with us." I was to leave with my youngest brother David for Israel. They assured me that my uncle Benny (Benjamin) will be like a father to us. Benny was single and lived with Granma where we would be staying.

When I discussed the matter with my mentors, including a physics teacher, they all agreed that going to Israel might be an excellent idea.

Everyone liked Israel in those days and even Muslims at times praised the Israeli courage and the famous one-eyed soldier (General Moshe Dayan).

My parents were sending me as a visitor to study at the university while my brother would attend a school on a Kibbutz. (A Kibbutz was a farming co-operative and there were about two hundred of them in Israel at the time. They were socialist entities where people's rank and education did not matter. They were all treated the same.)

It seemed the decision was made for me. We started the preparation for the trip.

My rich cousins and their parents showered me with gifts to take with me. The greatest gift came from their Grandpa (Monsieur Shalom), who gave me a small all silk Persian carpet and wished me success.

It wasn't easy to say goodbye to my uncle or to the Major. Since we didn't know when we will see each other again I remember both telling me "Don't forget us." There was no need to say goodbye to the rich

Cousins since they constantly visited Israel as well as some European countries.

The only other major issue was Shahin.

I called her out of her house for a walk and said to her: "I have been in love with you for these almost past five years hoping that someday you would have told me how you love me as well."

I went on: "Do you love me a bit?" I asked. No answer.

I now found enough courage to tell her this was where it ended for now. I explained how I am going to the unknown and how I didn't have any idea what lay ahead. I suggested we leave it to fate. We will meet and join hands in the future if that is what fate had for us. I also asked her not to see me off at the airport the next morning. I simply wanted to spare myself.

She simply kept her head down and went back to her house.

I must admit there was an air of freedom from slavery in what I had done. I still loved her but I was not settling for life in limbo.

She was there at the airport among the other well-wishers. My heart was pounding but I somehow was in control.

My brother and I boarded an El-Al plane. Smiling hostesses helped the passengers to their seats with the Word "Shalom."

The door was finally closed. There was a strange sense of pride in me when the pilot spoke in Hebrew on the speaker. A feeling you have when you are among the family. I belonged to a people.

# Chapter 16

# Arriving in Israel

# Chapter 16

# Arriving in Israel

Approaching Lod airport, we heard the Israeli national anthem on the speaker followed by well-wishing words of the captain informing us of our arrival to the Promised Land.

Everyone rushed to the windows for a glimpse of the land and the sea.

Many passengers, mostly new immigrants, got on their knees giving thanks for having seen such a day.

It was interesting to see almost all men dressed in khaki pants with a pulled up sleeve shirt in blue or in white waiting to receive relatives and friends on the tarmac. Most wore biblical sandals which consisted of one leather strip covering part of their toes.

I recognized my uncle through pictures he had sent us to Iran before. He was a handsome man. He looked like the famous Swiss actor Maximilian Schell. He was waving at us through the crowd. After an emotional greeting, he took us to a table where we were offered a glass of squeezed orange juice compliments of a Kibbutz which was trying to attract young newcomers to join their entity. The attendants were beautiful girls dressed in sexy shorts with a wide smile on their faces.

Note: Kibbutzim (plural of Kibbutz) were communal farms where people regardless of rank or education did all types of work by rotation in return for food, clothing, shelter and education. They enjoyed of all except money. It was a true form of socialism which according to Gorbachev only worked in Israel. There

Were about two hundred of them and in dire need of recruits. To a great extent, they were responsible for the amazing progress in Israel.

I was excited and astonished at changes from one country to another while on the bus to Jerusalem. The radio programs and songs were in Hebrew. People spoke a beautiful Hebrew which almost sounded like a European tongue. Their accent was totally different to that which we had been taught at the Jewish school.

To give an example: we had learned to say "shalum" while here they said "shalom." We committed this mistake with every word which had the letter. All in all, the Hebrew we spoke sounded funny and soon I would see how Israelis made fun of Persian Jews when they spoke Hebrew. It surely sounded funny.

The road to Jerusalem was like climbing a mountain, affecting our ears. I now knew why the bible says "You shall go up to Jerusalem" rather than going to Jerusalem.

We finally reached home to the eager arms of Grandmother and my young aunt. We hadn't seen each other for some twelve years. My brother and I felt most welcome. They couldn't stop pleasing us. My aunt moved to Granma's room and gave us hers as ours.

It was like another planet. Everything was simple. No one felt beneath the other and all saluted and acted with each other, as long as they were Eastern European or Israeli born, in an equal manner regardless of profession or wealth.

Here, everything was simplified and functional. Efficiency was seen in every turn.

Food was also a simple element. An egg sandwich in the morning followed by humus or falafel in a pita bread for lunch followed with salad and a small piece

Of fish or chicken with lots of bread for dinner. Red meat was a luxury.

People mostly kept their doors open and welcomed any stranger in need.

They called each other "friend" whenever stopped by someone for a question or directions.

It was during the third day of my arrival when I saw General Moshe Dayan (the one eyed general who was world famous) getting out of a car on the Jaffa road. It was hard to believe that I was feet away from this great warrior. He was dressed unimpressively in khaki pants and wore the normal biblical sandals. No one rushed to him for a kiss or a signature. People just said Shalom to him and passed him by.

Everyone was dressed in a simple manner but I still looked like a tourist. I had to have a change of attire. It was then that I collected my nerves and asked my uncle to lend me some money till I found a job.

He laughed saying: "I will take care of you for now till you are fully settled" and made it clear that I won't owe him anything. He was more generous than a father to both my brother and me.

He bought us clothing, shoes and took us on a tour of several cities where we had relatives and friends of the family. I know for a fact that he spent most of his savings if not all on both of us just to make sure we were happy. He never accepted anything in return.

It was time to get down to business. He enrolled my brother at a school on a Kibbutz where my brother was provided with all his necessities free of charge.

As for me, he enrolled me at a Hebrew school called Ulpan Etzion, designed to teach Hebrew in an accelerated fashion so that new immigrants could be immersed in the economic life as fast as possible. He paid for my room and board and asked me to learn as

Much as possible since the university classes would start in less than four months.

Ulpan Etzion was run by an American Zionist (Dr. Komrat) who had moved to Israel to serve the people. He was pleasant, kind and became emotional each time he saw a young Jew arriving in Israel.

I was given an entrance exam and put in the third grade. School had six grades altogether.

This was the first time I attended a co-ed school. There were boys and girls of my age and older all sharing classrooms together. They had come from every corner of the globe but were mostly Americans and Latin Americans with a few Persians like me. My roommate was an Argentinean who helped me with my homework whenever he wasn't spending time with his girlfriend away from school.

I studied hard all week and went to Granma for the weekends when I enjoyed of homemade cooking and lots of motherly love. It was certainly a new life.

I mostly mingled with students from America and from European countries since it was difficult to be accepted by the Israeli born boys and girls of my age.

The Israeli born had an air of superiority over the newcomers to the land. They had no complexes and felt free. They had no idea of anti-Semitism except what they had learned from their parents and from books. Their nickname was "Sabra," which is the cactus fruit. It meant they are tough and yet sweet. They all had one thing in common: they could hardly wait to join the army to the point that they even tried to lie about their ages to be recruited earlier. I rarely spoke to them for the fear that they might laugh at my accent.

I continued socializing with foreign students and tourist alike and finally got to know a woman in a biblical way for the first time. She was a twenty-nine

Years old tourist from Italy with whom I had a great time for about a month till she left Israel.

I finally started making some money at night by cleaning and washing new apartments ready for new immigrants to move in. This was a great help because now I was able to buy a pipe, a plastic overcoat and even take girls out for a movie or a falafel sandwich.

After being upgraded twice, I finally finished all six grades and was ready for enrollment at a university.

My uncle inquired about my field of interest. My answer was clear: engineering. He disagreed. He firmly believed in my leadership qualities. His reasoning was that all engineers end up working under someone who had studied economics and business.

He further believed that an engineer was simply a white collar worker and no more.

This was bizarre! I had been told all my young life how engineering is the answer for a bright future and now was being introduced to a new concept. It was almost like a sacrilege not to study engineering. My uncle and I had a long conversation but he finally convinced me to try economics for a year to see how I felt about this field. He assured me that Hebrew university requires a lot of math even in the field of economics which would help me change fields if I decided to after one year. He had convinced me.

My uncle Benny was an instructor in chemistry at the Hebrew university and thus knew some people of importance at the place.

He arranged all my records and certificates in a folder and off we went to meet the Dean of Social Sciences at the Hebrew University of Jerusalem.

The Dean, a pleasant man of about sixty or so, warmly welcomed us in and looked through my folder thoroughly. I could tell he was happy with what he had seen through the smile which was appearing on his face.

He said: "Impressive" and suddenly started to speak to me in English, to which I responded accordingly. He smiled again and switched to Hebrew.

Half an hour into our meeting, he looked at my uncle and said: "I am impressed. This young man comes to us from Paras (Iran) and yet has done much more than those coming to us from western countries where students have vast resources for progress."

He offered me a full scholarship, knowing of my financial situation, as well as a nominal rent for staying at the dorm. In addition, he gave me credit towards English courses as well. He as well made it clear that I needed to study hard since only about 10% of first year students of economics usually passed the year to the second one.

I was pleased and grateful for his generosity but the idea of America, America was still a disturbance.

I reasoned with myself continuously about Israel being the right place for me. After all, I was a Jew who had waited 2000 years to have a country of my own again. I had my own language. I felt Israel was a big house where we all lived as one family. Or was it?

Here, no one called me a "dirty Jew" but the Eastern Europeans, mostly survivors of the Holocaust, looked down at Jews coming from Muslim countries. They held the good jobs while trivial work (mostly in construction) was set aside for their oriental Jewish brothers. The made fun of us at every opportunity and in short, referred to us as "black Jews." They married among themselves and looked down at a European marrying an oriental.

This saddened me. We had seen prejudice and ill treatment in our homelands and had accepted them. But couldn't accept them in my own land. Aren't we all brothers and sisters?

These European Jews still had the concentration camp identity numbers tattooed on their arms.

How could they be capable of having prejudice against their own?

On one hand I had sympathy for them. They had gone through hell and back at the hands of despicable Nazis. They had the right to be mad at the world and especially at those who stood by while these innocent people were burnt in the ovens. On the other hand, it was hard to believe the relation between European and oriental Jews.

I finally reached a conclusion: any people who have suffered like the European Jews need to be forgiven for any mischief they may commit.

NOTE: almost all problems between European and Oriental Jews were resolved by the late 1980s.

In time, there was an Iranian descent president, a chief of staff as well as many ministers among oriental Jews. Intermarriages among the two factions became standard. And oriental Jews were no longer considered second class citizens.

Personally speaking, I never had any problem with the European Jews since I spoke English and acted as aloof as the Israeli born to the point that often I was asked whether I came from Paris or Paras (Iran).

My only intimate relation with an Israeli girl was with a chubby blond soldier I picked up one night in Tel-Aviv. Her name was Ester (Etty).

We saw lots of each other on her days off till finally she told me she was in love with me.

At her insistence, I accepted an invitation for a Friday night at their house. I took some flowers for her

mother and a box of candies for Etty. After dinner, her
father asked me to join him for a chat in their garden.

He started by saying how Etty, an only child, was his
world and how he wished the best life for her. Then he
went to the punch line: "I would have never allowed my
daughter to get serious with an oriental Jew yet she seems
to be in love with you." He went on: "You are quite
different," he told me. I asked "How so?" He said "Well, you
are presentable, polite and studying at the university." I
told him there were many decent European boys studying
at the Hebrew university.
He said "Yes I know but my daughter wants you."

I felt sorry for the poor man. Her daughter had put him
on a test of his principles.

By turn, I told him how I appreciated his kindness but
that I was not ready to become serious for years to come.
Truth be told, I felt offended.

Here I was in a Jewish state with fellow Jews and yet I
was experiencing prejudice simply because I wasn't from
Eastern or Western Europe. Little they knew that I came
from a tolerant country with a great past in culture and the
defense of human rights.

When I got back to Jerusalem, I wrote a letter to Etty
telling her how sorry I was not to be able to continue my
relation with her and wished her good luck. All in all, I
was still in love with Shahin but no longer mad.

Etty wouldn't have it. She kept on coming to
Jerusalem time and again but my decision had been made.

There were about a hundred students in every class I
attended at the university with a high percentage of
foreign students. The Israeli students were about four
years older than the rest since they had to finish the army
services before pursuing a higher education.

They were a breed to be proud of. The army had made them mature and self-sufficient.

A few weeks later, I found a part time job as assistant gardener at the campus, which helped me pay dorm rental, followed by another part time job as a night watchman at the Botanic building two nights a week.

A new dormitory had been built and ready where I was given a chance to live with another student in a comfortable room with kitchenette and a small bathroom. I was asked whether I minded to room with an Israeli Arab. I said "No not at all." Later I realized I had been asked this question since most other students did not wish to have an Arab roommate.

NOTE: Israeli Arabs are those who decided to stay in Israel after the partition of Palestine by the United Nations in 1947. In spite of invitations by surrounding Arab armies who wanted these Arabs to join in the throwing of the Jews to the sea, they stayed put. As a result, they are considered full Israeli citizens in every aspect with representation at the Knesset (the Israeli parliament).

My roommate was Ibrahim with whom I established a friendship bond from the start.

He had excellent Hebrew and had come from his village to study law.

When I visited his family once on a weekend, his father warmly welcomed me and let me know that he now has an additional son. Me.

I was treated like a prince and promised to go back for more visits.

It didn't take long till Ibrahim and an oriental Jewish girl fell madly in love. They soon started talking of marriage, all the while the girl thinking Ibrahim to be an oriental Jewish boy.

"Ibrahim I beg you," I said "Please, you must tell her you are Muslim as soon as possible."

He was afraid she would reject him if she knew of his religion. My answer was: "She will find out anyway and then there would be bloodshed on your hands." He agreed to tell her the next time they met. I assured him that he wouldn't lose her if hers is real love and not a fishing rod for catching a husband.

I shall not forget the night Ibrahim reached the room crying and cursing Jews and Arabs alike. She had told him to disappear the moment he had told her of his religion. It took weeks to pacify and console him but the harm was done. A nice young man was hurt without a real good reason. This was and perhaps is the reality in the Middle East.

I now had practically what any young man wished to have in Israel. I was at the university, I had work and also had much fun and yet was not very happy but content.

I visited many a Kibbutz and saw real socialism at work. People regardless of rank and position did all sorts of works including dishwashing and the cleaning of the bathrooms. Yet it wasn't my cup of tea.

One day after visiting some relatives in Tel-Aviv I stopped cold when I saw the seal of the US consulate on a building on my way to the bus. Involuntarily, I stepped in and asked the clerk at the information desk about requirements for getting a tourist visa.

After a brief conversation, he asked me for my passport. He paged the passport until saw the canceled US visa. Looking at me he asked if I had committed a crime in Iran. I told him "No." he claimed not to have ever seen a canceled visa before.

Reluctantly he gave me a form to fill out and suggested that I would hear from them without giving me any hope.

Realizing there was no hope of going to America, I decided to accept my lot and do my best with what was at hand.

I studied hard and enjoyed political debates with professors and with classmates alike, as well as going to parties and working at two part time jobs.

My parents immigrated to Israel just about this time and insisted in living in Jerusalem as most oriental immigrants did. I befriended an immigration officer, "Shlomo," who pulled some strings to materialize my parents' wish.

Shlomo kept encouraging me to join his political party, which I kept resisting since I had more interest in diplomacy than in domestic politics.

My parents together with my other two siblings were given a two room asbestos apartment, which was a normal government issue for the immigrants while waiting for an apartment, which was given free to each family. My father could not find a job since he had no technical trade but was finally able to find work at a post office selling stamps and other postal material.

I was desperate at not being able to help them financially but did what I could.

School year was coming to an end. I continued with my two jobs saving some money

As well as helping my family.

One night, when I opened my mail box at the dorm, I was astonished to see an envelope addressed to me and sent from the US consulate. I opened it hurriedly just to have my heart to stop. What a surprise! I had been granted a US tourist visa good for thirty days.

It couldn't be. It must have been a mistake. I looked at the envelope again. There was no mistake. It had been addressed to me. It was simply unbelievable.

That night, time and again I red the letter which said "We are pleased to inform you that you have been granted a visa and need to come to Tel-Aviv to have it sealed in your passport."

I was getting to love Israel and now this. Maybe I forget about America, I thought.

I thought and contemplated again and again till reaching the following conclusion:

I will have a faster personal growth if I went to America and surely will come back to Israel more marketable as far as a good job was concerned. So that was it.

When I finally calmed myself down, I realized I had two huge dilemmas: how do I find the money for such an expensive trip and where do I stay since my cousin in California was no longer an option. He had finished his studies and had returned to Tehran, where he got married and found a good job.

It seemed I needed a miracle again.

# Chapter 17

# The trip to America

# Chapter 17

## The trip to America

I fasted the night before going to the US consulate and practically prayed all night that the letter was not a joke but real.

Early in the morning, I got on the bus to Tel-Aviv, in fasting, with my body shaking till I got to the consulate.

The clerk asked for my passport and ten minutes later came back with a sealed tourist visa in my passport. I spoke none. Just thanked him and got out as fast as I could hoping that no one will call me back to cancel my visa.

Once on the street, I continuously looked back to make sure no one followed me while walking fast to the bus station. No one was following me!

I returned to Jerusalem hungry and now worrying about the trip. Where do I get the money I need? How much is the least I need? My problem was the amount I needed to pay for the ticket. As far as where to stay once in America, I was assured by a friend that I could stay with his friend Michael who was from Esfahan for at least a few days in Queens, New York. In other words, I was to drop on him without knowing much about him yet I knew the family he came from. I was going to be a real Chutzpa.

Air line prices of tickets from Israel to New York were prohibitive. I simply had to find the cheapest way to get there. It took a week of long hours and hard work to come up with the cheapest way to get to New York:

A boat ride to Cyprus then a third class ship ticket to Athens. From Athens, the cheapest train ticket to Luxemburg via Yugoslavia and Germany.

Luftlieder, Luxemburg air line, still used four engine planes thus offering the cheapest way to New York via air.

So that was the plan. I got my membership card to youth hostels from the student union as well as an international driver's license from the motor vehicle department.

For the next two months, I saved every penny I could working two and three part time jobs yet I was still short three hundred dollars to cover the trip. There was no one who could help or lend me this sum. I sat on my bed thinking and thinking till it finally hit me.

I suddenly remembered the small silk Persian rug Monsieur Shalom had given me in Tehran as a going away present. That was it. I needed to sell it. After trying several stores, I was able to sell it for three hundred fifty dollars. I now had enough to cover my trip and have an extra fifty dollars for food during my long trip. Next, I made sure to have the necessary visas for countries which I would be passing through. They all told me there was no need of acquiring any visa since I would be in transit.

My parents had not much to say except wishing me well and repeatedly telling me not to forget my brothers. They made it clear, as was the oriental custom, that I must help my siblings once on my feet.

The separation from my Uncle Benny and from Granma was an emotional one as well.

My uncle slipped a twenty dollar bill in my hand and asked me not to forget to visit Columbia University as well as Yeshiva University once in New York. He took me to the port of departure while repeatedly reminding me that leaders mostly come from those who study business and economics.

The trip to Cypress and to Athens was uneventful, I mostly stayed on the deck staring at the waves and thinking what the future might have in the bag for me.

I was on the train in Athens on my way to Luxemburg just a few hours after my arrival in the Greek city.

My fellow passengers were mainly from Greece, Turkey and Yugoslavia. Most were on their way to Germany where they worked in construction or as house maids.

I sat next to a middle aged man from Turkey who spoke just a few words in English.

I noticed how he couldn't stop looking at a blond woman seated near us while playing with his worry beads hurriedly and anxiously. It was about an hour into the trip when he finally could not tolerate the situation. He begged me in broken English to ask the blond as to how much he would need to pay her parents
for her hand. I was surprised!

Repeatedly, I told him Europeans don't understand customs as such but to no avail.

I couldn't stop laughing at his seriousness about the issue, I gave up.

I approached the woman who turned out to be from Yugoslavia and told her about the man seated next to me. We both laughed for a moment. It was then that she asked me if I thought my friend was a rich man. I said I guess so.

She agreed to see him and spend some time with him once they reached their mutual destination. She also asked me to let the man know that she doesn't come cheap!

I conveyed the message to the man who by hearing the result, hugged and kissed me and gave me a five dollar bill as my reward.

We arrived in Ljubljana (a Yugoslavian city with magnificent scenery) on a Friday early afternoon. After some disembarked and others came aboard, an inspector came aboard to inspect our passports. After checking my passport, he informed me that I need to get off and acquire a transit visa for Luxemburg!

I tried to explain to him how I had checked with pertinent consulates in Jerusalem and how they had told me there would be no need for visas. He wouldn't have it. I kept on insisting with no success. He finally ordered me off the train.

The trains disappeared from sight while I stood by the tracks with my suitcase wondering what to do or where to go. To make matters worse, I was told that all consulates close Friday mid-day till Monday morning.

Carrying my heavy suitcase, I walked towards what seemed to be a main avenue like a zombie. I stopped every person I passed by and asked him or her if they spoke English.

The answer was always the same. No.

Carrying the heavy suitcase was giving me a backache. I wandered to a park and sat on a bench catching my breath while asking the same question like a broken record: do you speak English? The answer continually was No.

About an hour later I saw a young man of about my age passing through. He spoke English! Smilingly he said his name was Boris. I explained my dilemma about the visa as well as not knowing where to stay till Monday morning. I asked if he knew of any youth hostels. "You won't need a hostel," Boris suggested. I asked "Then where do I go?"

It turned out that his father was a professor at the University and thus Boris knew some people there who could, at his request, help me with a roof over the weekend.

I couldn't believe what was happening. Was Boris an angel in form of a young man?

Surely he was a G-d sent.

He helped me with the suitcase till we reached the beautiful campus of Ljubljana University. Once we reached the dormitory, he spoke to a clerk who smiled and shook his head in a positive way.

The man led us to a room in the building. Boris explained to me that there are two Palestinian students who dorm in this room but one is away for the weekend and that I could have his bed. Boris made sure I was comfortably placed and promised to see me for breakfast the next day.

My roommate was a Palestinian student! I knew immediately that I must not engage in any conversation about Israel and speak only about Iran.

We conversed about politics till late in the night. He had tearful eyes when he showed me a picture of his village which by now was a part of Israel.

His parents had been among Palestinian Arabs who had left Israel after the partition following Arab propaganda against the newly formed state of Israel. They had fled hoping that soon after they would attack Israel and push the Jews to the sea.

That night when I was finally ready to go sleep taking my shirt off, I suddenly remembered my Star of David necklace around my neck. In a split second, I ripped the chain and took the necklace off wrapped in my shirt.

I spent the rest of that weekend with Boris, who showed me museums and parks. He even brought me a hat as a gift. When I asked what he would want me to send him from America, he begged for a record from Frank Sinatra. Four months later I sent him three of Sinatra's latest records.

Boris took me to the consulate first thing in the morning on Monday and saw me off at the train station. It was then that I started believing that angels come in all forms.

I arrived at Luxemburg airport two hours before the flight to New York.

A ground hostess at the desk informed me of a thirty five dollar refund due to me due to seasonal change of fares. Realizing how badly my parents needed money, I asked her to send it to my parents' address.

Next to me on the plane sat a Mr. Cohen who was partially blind and he told me of his sufferings during the Holocaust and about the concentration camp he had been at. He was very sympathetic and offered me to stay in his apartment in Manhattan where he lived with his wife and son if I would need a place to stay for a while. He insisted the offer was good should I not find the friend who lived in Queens hospitable.

Mr. Cohen was very helpful. He taught me how avenues and streets run in Manhattan as well as giving me the names of various Jewish organizations that might be of assistance.

He also mentioned Yeshiva University and suggested I pay a visit as well.

We landed about six in the afternoon at Kennedy airport and, surprisingly enough, I went through the customs clearance without any problems. Once outside, I started asking for the bus stop and soon was on Q-10 bus on my way to Queens.

I had finally arrived in America with a total of thirteen dollars in my pocket and a suitcase of books and clothing.

# Chapter 18

# Arriving at my friend's Apartment

# Chapter 18

## Arriving at my friend's apartment

I knocked on the door with palpitating heart. It was Morad who opened the door. There was no need for any introduction since we immediately recognized each other. We both had studied at the same Jewish elementary school.

He welcomed me in while introducing me to his roommate, who was an Iranian boy as well. After I refreshed myself, Morad told me that I can sleep in the corner of their living room since they had no extra room in the apartment. The boys couldn't believe that I had landed with only thirteen dollars.

While sitting to dinner, Morad recommended that I should find a job as busboy in a restaurant as soon as possible. I assured them both that I will not disturb them but for a few days till I find a job.

While at dinner, I realized that there was not enough bread and offered to go down to the street and buy some if they could give me the direction to a store. It was at this point that my friend's roommate devastated me with his words. He said: there is enough bread if I could eat like a human being but not enough if I usually eat like an animal. I was shocked. But couldn't bring myself to answer him and instead just got up telling them I had terrible stomach ache probably due to the strange food on the plane and needed to get some sleep.

I went to sleep crying with a stomach ache due to hunger. It was scary. I was moneyless and alone in a new land. Why did I leave Israel? I kept asking myself.

That night, my grandfather came to my dream saying: "Don't worry, my boy" holding my hand while walking on a street till he stopped, asking me to look up and look at a building which simply said 'Yeshiva.' He told me to go in at which moment I woke up sweating. Somehow, I knew my grandfather was trying to help me from above.

It was about five in the morning when I got up dressed and made up my mind to pursue the dream I had had a few hours ago. Suddenly it dawned on me. Mr. Cohen had spoken to me about Yeshiva University on the plane. Therefore, the word Yeshiva I had seen in my dreams had to do with the conversation on the plane. Leaving a note for my hosts, I left about seven and after hurriedly buying and devouring Italian bread went down to the subway station asking the man in the booth how to get to Yeshiva University.

Realizing I am a stranger, he taught me how to call information for free from a public phone to get the address I needed. With an address in my hand I purchased a token for fifteen cents and was on my way to my destination. I had read about the building of the New York subway but now I had a chance to respect and salute the blood and sweat of the Irish immigrants who had been responsible for this wondrous work.
While at the same time admiring American ingenuity.

Changing trains at Times Square, I finally arrived in Washington Heights in lower Manhattan. Crowded streets, bustling stores and fast walking people astonished me. After asking for directions several times, I finally arrived at Yeshiva University. It was strange to see so many boys with small caps, kipa, on their heads rushing in and out of different buildings. The first thing entering my mind was imagining Jewish boys walking with a kipa on their head in a Muslim country! This made me to laugh immediately.

I was able to figure out which was the administrative building and walked in while mentioning the name of G-d in my heart.

"Shalom," I said to a well dressed man with a hat on who promptly said "Shalom" with smile. Once I explained my situation to him in a nutshell, he suggested I should see Dr. Greenstein, showing me the way to his office.

Dr. Greenstein's secretary (Sarah) wanted to know why I need to see the doctor since I wasn't a student at the school.

Seeing my desperation, she finally agreed to see if her boss would see me for a few minutes.

She came back from his office with a smile telling me that Dr. Greenstein will see me shortly.

With a kipa on my head (as per tradition, Jewish boys of Esfahan always carried a kipa in their pocket) I entered the office saying "Shalom, Doctor," at which he nodded his head and signaled me to sit down.

After hearing my story, he smiled and said "I have to give it to you. You are courageous but there is no way you can make it."

He went on explaining the problems I would face for not having some money as well as a necessary student visa. Dr. Greenstein volunteered to make a few phone calls to see if he could get enough money to buy me a one way ticket to Israel.

I kept on insisting to him that all I needed was a chance. Finally and smilingly he agreed to help but after my school grades had been examined by the office of the registrar.

As part of the agreement, I was supposed to get a job and a place to live at.

I agreed and asked him for a maximum of ten days to do so and if failed, then I will be most grateful for that one way ticket back to Israel. Before I left for the

177

office of admission, the good man gave me a signed note good for two meals at the university cafeteria. He further instructed Sarah to show me the board where Jewish families advertised to let rooms to the students of Yeshiva. I kissed his hands and thanked him repeatedly.

Looking at the board, I found one which was nearest to the campus. It belonged to a Mrs. Bernstein. When I knocked on her door, an old sweet looking and short lady opened the door. She looked at me for a few moments before she asked me if I was a Yeshiva boy. I said "Yes."

She directed me to a room which looked quite large, furnished with a comfortable looking bed. As I sat on the bed to test the mattress, she sat next to me with wet eyes saying her husband had died on this bed six months ago. I jumped off the bed scared but was not in a position to be choosy.

We agreed on seven dollars per week. I paid her an initial four dollars while she agreed to have me move in immediately and pay the rest of the rent by the weekend.

I picked up my suitcase from Morad's apartment and moved in by late afternoon.

I was finally able to take a real shower but couldn't fall asleep easily knowing that my landlord had passed away on this same bed. I thought, what if he came back? I finally fell asleep hoping I would find a job by tomorrow. Mrs. Bernstein woke me up quite early offering me breakfast (she really had rented the room to fight loneliness so I was now like a grandson living with Granma).

I started walking on the street going from store to store asking for a job of any kind but no one had any opening.

After several hours of walking, my feet were hurting and my moral was even worse. After hours of walking the streets and begging for a job, I entered Dykeman Street. The beautiful and large bakery in the corner must have had a magnetic force or else I was simply starved.

It was called Regina Bakery. The man and woman working together behind the counter seemed to be man and wife.

I bought a roll of bread and depressively asked if they had an opening. The man behind the counter looked at my kipa on my head and presently said, "No I have nothing suitable for a Yeshiva boy." "But, Sir, I would do anything. I really need a job."

Suddenly the lady (his wife) who had heard it all approached me. "Boychic, you really need a job don't you?" she asked.

I practically screamed: "Yes, yes I desperately need a job and don't care what I have to do. I will even clean the bathrooms if the job calls for that."

She went on: "What I have is not for a Yeshiva boy but you are welcome to it if you so badly need a job."

My task was to wash the sticky floors and baking trays and appliances from four thirty after midnight to seven in the morning. I couldn't conceal my happiness.

She showed me the products which were made with water or with vegetable oil and told me: "Don't over work yourself and eat whatever you want and as much as you want. Her action made me homesick for my mother. This lady was really acting like a mom.

I now had only about four dollars to my name but was equipped to go forward. Both Mrs. Bernstein as well as Regina Bakery treated me well. It was a week later when I earned my first thirty dollars. It looked like a million.

It was time to buy some clothing since my attire consisted of used clothing I had bought from an American student at the Hebrew University of Jerusalem who was returning home to the USA. I also needed a transistor radio for some kind of entertainment but first I had to get a Social Security number, which I did.

Next, I put a pair of pants and two shirts on lay away and bought a radio for eight dollars. The first song I heard on my transistor was "You've Lost that Loving Feeling" by the Righteous Brothers, which remains one of my most favorite songs to date.

I visited Dr. Greenstein early Monday morning. He was pleased with my accomplishments and promised to help me with a scholarship due to my grades of the past three years. In fact, I was given twelve free credits due to the amount of mathematic courses I had taken up to that time.

I was to take a course in Jewish studies for the rest of that semester till the new one when I would carry seventeen credits at Yeshiva College for secular studies while taking the same number of credits in the Teacher's Institute of Jewish studies simultaneously. This was the regular load at the Yeshiva College for men for the first four years of college education. In other words, each student carried thirty-four credits each semester.

This was a welcome decision. I needed to learn about Judaism in a logical and analytical way. Until then, I was a Jew simply because I had been born a Jew.

Now I had a chance to learn more and not in a fundamentalist way but with an open mind.

Next I was sent to Rabbi Dobrinsky, a very kind man, who later found a prominent Iranian Jew who

180

agreed to be my guarantor while studying in college, through which I was granted a student visa.

Life was becoming more normal and with less anxiety.

My daily program was a routine now; early morning to work then to school till late in the evening then homework till fairly late. Once in a while, I would go to the student hall to watch the then popular Batman show on TV.

I constantly questioned my teachers about different points in Judaism and was always insistent about comparative analysis among the three religions. In particular, with Islam, since more and more I saw many common points and even laws in both religions. So what was going on? Judaism had come first so was it that the other two religions took the best of Judaism and evolved with time?

The teachers answered my questions in earnest and would also at times recognize they did not have an answer. I admired their truthfulness; they were all religious but a vanguard at the same time.

To mingle with the Yeshiva boys was a difficult task. They were all decent, polite and had one thing on their mind. To excel. They studied hard causing a tremendous competitiveness which often forced professors to grade exams on a curve where an A would become a C+. They had no time for socializing except maybe on Saturday night after sundown. They were all well provided for by their families with no worries at all. Even their laundry was done by Mom when they went home for the weekend. Of course, there were some students from outside of the States but their needs were fully taken care of by their parents.

Soon I became very friendly with two boys from out of state. One was Richard and the other Izzy. We often went to Greenwich Village on Saturday nights to have some fun and meet girls if possible since Yeshiva College was for men only.

We met very interesting people there and had a great time observing the hippies and their way of life. Some of the musicians we saw there later became quite famous nationwide.

Sometimes, I spent the night at the dorm with my two friends talking about our encounters, life in Iran and future plans.

Once in a while I was invited to a Jewish family for Sabbath through a program designed by the university to make foreign students feel at home. They were always kind and made one feel like a member of the family. Sometimes they would go as far as putting a few dollars in my pocket for the trip expense to their home.

Passover was approaching. My two friends informed me kosher hotels in upstate New York had sent people to the university to hire some boys to work as waiters and busboys at their hotels during the holidays. The three of us got a job at the same hotel. This became quite an experience to remember. We worked hard serving three meals a day to the same families for about eight days. Often towards the end of dinner the mother at the table would force us to sit and eat something regardless of the fact that we were not allowed to do so. Her answer was always "Let somebody say something to me and he will see what
would happen to him."

In other words, we were like her sons and she was upset to see us work so hard. Thank goodness for mothers.

After work, we had quite a field day but in a most decent manner. Three dashing young men with one problem; which girl to choose to socialize with? As difficult as it was, we never forgot which school we were from.

On the last day, we were given extremely generous tips with the mandatory promise that we will visit the families every chance we would get.

Wow. I had made five hundred dollars in one week. To me, it looked like a great deal of money.

We had had so much fun that I thought we should have been charged and yet they had paid us. Once back, I opened a saving account and sent more than half to my parents.

New semester was about to start which meant carrying thirty-four credits per semester. Half in Jewish studies while the other half in secular courses. This meant that I no longer could work at the bakery. I carefully arranged the timing of some courses so that I could have a few free hours during the afternoon to find a part time job.

# Chapter 19

# Life at Yeshiva University

# Chapter 19

# Life at Yeshiva University

Unlike normal colleges, Yeshiva students had to carry
seventeen credits in Jewish studies and another
seventeen in the secular field of their choice.
Remembering the words of my Uncle Benjamin, I chose
economics and math as my secular field. I still needed a
job. Mr. Parker, who was in charge of all Yeshiva
University cafeterias offered me a job as a server at Stern
College cafeteria (Yeshiva college for women). Being a
part time job it didn't pay much but was enough to carry
me through. It was also a big boost to my ego. Imagine all
those young ladies flirting with me.

I went out with several but they all had one thing on
their mind: marriage.

I paid all my attention to science courses and did not
take economics seriously, so much so that I ended
receiving an F in that course. That did it. Economics now
became a challenge.

As summer approached, I started looking for a full
time job. After looking around and also going to
employment agencies I landed a job at College Corner
Coffee Shop located close to New York University in the
Village. I made quite good money working as a waiter
and enjoyed the Village atmosphere as well. My day
started at about 6 AM and I worked till three in the
afternoon.

Arriving early one Sunday morning, while waiting for
the owner of the coffee shop to arrive, a young girl about
my age, running towards the shop, stopped a few

steps from me asking if I had seen a boy about my age and somewhat dark waiting around the shop. At first I thought she was trying to be funny since she was almost describing me. I asked her laughingly: "You sure it is not me?"

She laughed back and said "No. He is a foreign student from Jordan who is supposed to meet me here with other students to go to the United Nations building for a tour." I politely answered "No I have seen no one." Next she asked me if I were an Arab. To which I firmly answered "No." when she heard I was a Jewish boy coming from Israel her eyes lit up and she asked what I was doing there so early. I was answering her when the Arab boy appeared. Before she left, she asked me till what time was I working while waving goodbye.

It was about two thirty in the afternoon when I saw her waving at me through the window. She came in, sat at my counter saying "Hi. My name is Tania." I promptly introduced myself and offered her a cold drink. She wanted to go for a walk after I was done with work, to which I agreed.

We started walking towards Washington Square. She wanted to know all about a Kibbutz (a rural community—Israel has about 200 of them), student life and more in Israel.

In fact, she seemed obsessed with Israel.

She turned out to be a Jewish girl born to a Polish Jewish family in Colombia. She had wanted to emigrate to Israel at seventeen, going to a Kibbutz, but her parents adamantly stopped her fearing that she might become a Communist if they allowed her to go. I could easily see that she was in the US physically but lived in Israel mentally. Her parents had tried everything to make her forget her idea but with no success. Now she was enrolled at New York University by her parents, living at the dorm with all expenses paid. Her parents

188

had promised to review their decision about her going to Israel once she graduated from college.

I also told her about my life and adventures and also how I would want to get a few degrees, work in the US for a while and then go back.

She was a charming girl with a nice figure. We spent the whole afternoon. She gave me her phone number and I gave her the number of the public phone, the only phone available to me, on the dorm floor of my buddies at Yeshiva. Each time I wanted to leave she asked me to stay another hour. I finally left the Village about ten in the evening.

Next evening, I heard my name called out while I was in a friend's room at the dorm. I had a call. It was her.

When I said hello her first words were: "I can't wait till Sunday to see you." I explained to her about my school load and how it was difficult for me to be out often. She didn't agree and was quite upset yet there wasn't much I could do. I wasn't in love and she wasn't the only girl I was in touch with.

I was coming out of my physics lab on Wednesday at 9 PM when I saw her sitting on one of the dorm steps with what seemed to be a wrapped gift under her arm.

"I missed you very much" she said offering me the gift.

I accepted the gift thanking her. I was thrilled to see someone should care so much as to go through the trouble of coming downtown late at night just to see me.

After seeing her off at the subway, I started thinking. Was she in love with me? She was a good girl. The kind Jewish mothers want for their sons. Jewish, virgin and loving. She was all Mom had ordered me to look for.

The question was whether I was ready for a steady commitment. After all, I was quite popular and had a number of girls around me.

We agreed to see each other at least twice a week. But soon that wasn't enough since I was also falling for her.

It devastated me when I found out that she had participated in a medical test as a guinea pig to make some money with which she had bought me gifts. I now had no doubt that she was in love with me.

We had known each other for six months when she told me of her mother's hopeless sickness. The lady had cancer and wasn't expected to live much longer. She went on saying that her parents wanted to meet me but due to her mother's health it was not possible to come to New York.

It was at this point that she showed me a round trip ticket to Bogotá drawn to my name. Her parents had invited me to go and spend a few days with them. I was overwhelmed. It was then that I found out that she comes from a well to do household.

I politely asked her to hold on to the ticket just for a day or two till I consult some people. She agreed but hoped that I would take the trip with her.

My next stop was the office of Dr. Greenstein.

"My boy they wouldn't have sent you a ticket if they didn't have some serious thoughts about your relation with their daughter." He believed that they may ask me to marry her.

"What should I do, doctor?" I asked.

His answer was: "You must make the final decision. Go if you are serious about this girl."

Both my friends were against the trip. They were sure I would come back married. I simply laughed at them. How could I get married now? I still have so much study and work ahead.

When I approached Tania with the above results she simply cried and suggested I really didn't love her.

It saddened me to see a girl who is about to lose her mother cry. I finally kissed her and agreed on the trip. I kept on wondering why everyone believes that I will end up married if took the trip. I was simply going to meet my girl's parents.

Tania would not move out of my arms during the entire flight. We were like two love birds attracting the attention of smiling passengers aboard.

We finally landed. Tania was waving at two men standing on the tarmac through the window. The two men were her father, Mr. Manuel, and her second brother, Leon.

I was warmly welcomed by both once on the ground. I must admit of my high regards for the father before even meeting him.

He had left Poland at seventeen alone in search of a new life.

Upon his arrival in Colombia he had started working as a peddler working his way up and up. Once established, he had asked for the hand of his niece (a most beautiful girl) whom his sister had sent to Colombia to marry him. This union did not seem strange to me at all since marrying a cousin was a respected and welcome union in Iran throughout centuries.

We were ushered to a beautiful Lincoln Continental with a uniformed chauffer on our way home. I think it was then that I realized of my new relation with a real rich family. I was scared. I wondered, will I be able to handle myself correctly?

Will I know enough about the rules of etiquette?

For now I kept busy looking at the streets and so many churches through the car window. It was Leon who saw my astonishment at seeing so many churches.

Presently in a most eloquent English he informed me that Colombia is the most Catholic country in the world.

The car finally went through what seemed to be a very affluent neighborhood and turned into the driveway of what seemed to be a mansion.

"We are home," said Tania. I was in awe.

# Chapter 20

# Arriving in Bogotá, El Dorado

# Chapter 20

## Arriving in Bogotá, El Dorado

I couldn't believe my eyes when I entered the house: an internal garden larger than many external ones I had seen with rooms all around it romancing a curved staircase introducing one to the second floor. I was admiring the house when Tania broke in: "Come let's go and say hello to my mother," she said.

I entered a large room nicely decorated with what seemed to be expensive furniture and ornaments.

A most elegant blond lady with blue eyes was sitting on the bed with a smile on her face.

Tania jumped into her arms while I bent my head saluting her.

She signaled me to approach her and offered me her face to kiss which I did excitedly. She welcomed me warmly and after a short chat suggested I go and get some rest before dinner.

Although the family wanted me to get some rest, Tania insistently wanted to stay with me in my room.

Later I was asked to review the flowers sent to the house by family and friends welcoming me to Bogotá.

There must have been at least sixteen people invited to the first dinner. This became the norm during my short stay in Colombia. There were three servants, each assigned to a different task, while also a nurse for the mother.

We all went to a country club where the family had membership on Sunday. What a place, what a royal treatment. This was all too much for a poor boy to digest. I was simply in Utopia.

To Mr. Manuel's astonishment, Tania and I were in each other's arms kissing and hugging.

It was in the afternoon of the next day when Tania's father called me to his room with Leon as the interpreter.

He wanted to know what were my intentions with his daughter ?

I answered him in earnest. I said "Sir, I plan to get my first degree first and then marry your daughter while I will go on studying for a higher degree."

He stared at me for a few moments and finally concluded: "OK then Tania will stay here while you finish your education."

I agreed but also told him that it would be difficult not to see her for such a long while.

He suggested I would be provided with plane tickets to come and visit her once in a while. I agreed again. I had seen his point. He was afraid to send his daughter back with me without a proper union, fearing of the worst.

He even suggested that I could work with him once I got my degree, when I arrogantly told him no thanks since I intend to make it all on my own. Years later I realized what a mistake that had been since people think you get rich when you marry a rich girl regardless of whether you receive riches from them or not.

We hadn't finished talking when I heard Tania's cry from behind the door. She had heard it all. It turned out to be a sad afternoon.

Later when I was sitting on my bed, the mother, whom I affectionately called Dona Henia, entered my room. You could see she was in pain when she sat next to me combing my hair with her hand in a motherly way. She told me not to worry since she will have a talk with her husband hoping to change his mind about Tania staying home while I am gone.

She kissed my face and left the room. It broke my heart to see such a lovely person just waiting to die.

Here was a woman who had worked hard hand in hand with her husband for so many years. They had finally made it big and now, which was the time to pick the fruits of her labor, she was about to die. I couldn't help but remember the words of King Solomon when he said "Vanity of vanities, all is vanity."

Nothing is forever. Blessed is the person who lived well and enjoyed life while walking in the path of G-d.

It was finally Leon who changed the silence in the house by nightfall. He took me by the arm and led me to his room.

While crying hard he said "Listen, Yigal: I know Tania and you are in love." I said "Yes." He continued: "You know my mom will not last much longer and if so why not let her have a bit of joy before she leaves us?" I asked him what could we do?

"Why not marry now?" He asked "But Leon, how? I am a poor first year student studying in a new country. Besides, we are so young." "But you are planning to marry each other anyway," he said. I agreed but reminded him that we could do so once we are at least twenty-two with a diploma and a job.

Leaving my room he insisted that I should give it more thought.

I spent most of the night thinking in bed. What was I to do?

I was so young with so many plans before thinking of marriage. Was I selfish? On one hand I was trying to be logical while on the other I had to answer my heartache about their mother.

I felt like an egoist who was playing high and mighty. But that wasn't me. I finally gave up to myself.

I figured once married, we will go back to New York, rent a one bedroom apartment and I will work as a waiter while we both will continue our studies. I also figured that I must ask Mr. Manuel to pay for Tania's tuition at NYU since there was no way I could manage that. So that was it. I didn't need to ask my parents' opinion since I had been on my own since the age of fourteen. It was my decision and mine alone.

I knocked on Tania's room early next morning (she hadn't talked to me most of the day before). She started jumping with joy drowning me in kisses once she knew of my intention.

Her mother invited us both to her arms kissing and blessing us both. She was revived and on the phone making wedding arrangements minutes later.

They decided the wedding should be held at home inviting only about one hundred people since mother could not leave for outside.

On the wedding night, Tania called me over before the guests' arrival to a corner.

She wanted me to promise her that we would move to Israel as soon as possible. This looked strange although I knew of her love for life on a Kibbutz. I still sometimes think that one of the main reasons she married me was her hope of going to Israel as soon as she could.

Affectionately I told her how I must first finish my education, get experience and then we could move to Israel. She simply wanted a firm promise. So much so that she went on saying that was her condition. Kissing her, I said "I shall try my best."

Her parents offered us a paid honeymoon to any destination we would like. I politely refused and hours after the wedding we were on our way to New York in order not to lose any time from school. We got back to New York with about $5000 in wedding gifts. This sum was enough to secure us an apartment and have a good portion of it in a saving account.

We took a room in Hotel New Yorker for a few days while searching for a permanent place during our off hours.

I remember us both crying the first night sleeping in the same bed since we really didn't know what to do or what would be next.

Days later, to my dismay, Tania informed me how she will not pursue her college studies any longer. I could not convince her to go back regardless of how much I tried.

We finally found a studio at a residential hotel in Manhattan were we stayed the next six months.

Three months had passed when we were called to Bogotá to spend with my mother in law her last days with us.

I was sitting on her bed when she took her last breath.

Not only that it was a great loss but it was also the beginning of the family downfall.

My wife and I got back to New York a few days later, when Tania told me she was pregnant. How sad the mother didn't know when she left us.

Once her father found out, he had Tania move back to Colombia where she would be well taken care of. This meant that I had to stay alone back in New York to finish the semester, which I did, and join her in Bogotá.

Once in Bogotá, I enrolled at the Los Andes University while taking an accelerated Spanish course designed for diplomats.

I was now studying hard but had everything a person may need for a comfortable life and yet I missed New York.

During my stay in Colombia, I met many cultured and well to do people.

Mr. Sammy Rohr was among them, who soon took a liking to me and asked me to enter into one of his business ventures once back in the USA. He was a philanthropist who helped those in need. Don Sammy was my mentor for years to come until he passed away.

My first son, Yuri, was born in 1967. That brought a great deal of joy to the entire family.

I had finished the school year successfully and with mutual agreement was to go to New York to find an apartment so my wife and son could join me.

The idea of remaining in Colombia for good had entered my mind often but I couldn't accept it due to the social structure.

I could easily see a parallelism between Colombia and Iran.

Here too a small portion of the population was very rich while most others just struggled to survive. As a young idealist, I wondered why Communism had not arrived in this Latin American country. There was an answer to that: regardless of their hardships, they always had a smile on their faces, while being the most Catholic country also helped. The Bogotános, even the poor ones, were always impeccably dressed and were politically correct in their answers. For those two reasons, Bogotá was called the London of Latin America.

The coastal people were happier, less conservative and quite musical.

I had worked part time during the year in Bogotá and had found people to be very patient and hopeful about the future

Yet, as an idealist, I could not stomach the huge social differences.

While in Colombia, I tried to explain about Iran and Iranians.

I found the need to do so since to most Colombians Iran was still the land of "one thousand and one nights."

All in all, I have great memories of Colombia.

Had I known Colombia would evolve to a great economy and a democratic land, I might not have left at all. But at the time, I simply didn't want to live in a place like where I had come from only due to social injustices. The decision was made: we would go back to the USA.

# Chapter 21

# Back to New York

# Chapter 21

# Back to New York

Back in New York, I employed the help of a real estate lady who found me an apartment. She also lured me into breaking one of the commandments, which changed my life forever.

The guilt feeling was overwhelming.

I simply had to confess to my wife, who was witnessing changes in my behavior.

My confession resulted in twenty-five years of suffering for both of us till our marriage finally ended in a divorce.

My wife looked for any opportunity to take long trips taking the children with her while my life was becoming lonely accompanied by terrible migraine headaches.

I received my first degree in 1969 and was accepted by New York University to pursue my studies further towards an M.B.A.

I had always admired diplomacy. To that end, I approached the Iranian consulate to learn about a career in that field. I felt well equipped since by then I spoke four languages and had lived in three different countries. I was politely given a negative answer since by law an Iranian diplomat had to be a Muslim. Well, having been turned down, my plan was to get my next degree and climb the corporate ladder to an eventual high position. In the meantime, I continued working as a teacher combined with a weekend job selling jewelry. This combination was enough to carry the house expenses through.

My plans for the future took a curve once my brothers joined me with the hope of a better future. Although I tried my best for them to pursue a college career, they had no appetite for that since their mind was set on business.

According to my traditions and customs of where I came from, being the first born, I was responsible for my siblings.

This represented another matrimonial hardship. My wife, who came from a different set of customs and traditions could not understand my obsession about my brothers.

While continuing my graduate studies, I had to find a way for my two brothers to prosper towards a better future.

I received my M.B.A. in 1971 and soon became an American citizen. The MBA program had opened my focus. It was a relatively new field teaching new ways to corporate America where no longer a handful of CEOs made business out of favoritism or playing golf. It transfused fresh blood into the way business was to be conducted on the corporate level. Upon my graduation I found a job with a company on Lexington Avenue dealing with commodities worldwide. My first task was to develop a shrimp market for the company, a task which looked impossible since the Japanese had cornered the shrimp market all over Latin America. After a great deal of effort, I was able to find a small exporter in a far out corner of Colombia although we couldn't make any profit at the price we would buy the goods. After much talk, I convinced the CEO to let me buy and sell with no profit for a while promising him that it would be a profitable endeavor after a while. Three months down the line, I was able to develop such a relationship with my supplier that he (Don Arturo) had wanted to adopt me as his son. From then on, he dropped his price so that my company could profit from his shrimps. Unfortunately, I had stop working at the company since I needed to think of a business where my brothers would be involved as well. Being that Boutique business was a flourishing endeavor in the seventies, and through my wife's help, I opened a shop in the Bronx putting my brothers in charge. It was a success from day one prompting me to dream of a chain of boutiques nationwide. My wife again found it bizarre when I took my brothers as equal partners.

During a trip to Miami I realized the importance of the Latin influence in that city. This, coupled with my experience with Latin Americans in the Bronx led me to sign a lease in the newly developed Omni Mall. The entire family was against my decision and yet I knew this was a good step.

I had seen the rush of Venezuelan shoppers in Miami coupled with all the high rises appearing in every corner.

Single handedly I drove a truck load of clothing and equipment to Miami and opened the new shop. I was amazed. I was right. The tourists would buy anything and everything. So much so that within less than a week I was out of inventory. We opened two more stores within a year and seven more within the next three years ending up with eleven stores in malls all over Florida.

My wife's separation from me through frequent trips was becoming a way of life. To escape from reality I immersed myself in work but also started to enjoy the Miami night life when possible.

It was during the summer when Tania again asked for a divorce. My condition was always the same: leave my children and do as you wish. My children were my life, my raison d'être, which she knew.

We reached a compromise: she will take the children and live in Israel where she always had wanted to be while I visit them once every two months. This arrangement was an additional stress but was better than a divorce. To take advantage of these cumbersome and expensive trips, I started buying expensive clothing samples from Paris or Milan on my way to visit them, planning to copy them in Israel for our stores.

I found Gaza to be the most effective and most reasonable way of production.

I met Mahdi, a Palestinian, who was charming, friendly and most accommodating. His house was my house and his family was my family. So much affection and hospitality often made me sad and homesick for Iran.

It often reminded me of my Muslim friends and teachers in Esfahan. The Islam I knew was the way these teachers and friends had behaved with me without a single prejudiced bone in their bodies. This was the Islam I knew and with which I lived in harmony. Yes there was some prejudice here and there as in any land or country in the world.

I would look at Mahdi and think: why can't the Israelis and Arabs find a common ground? We are cousins after all. Why is it that the more civilized we become the more cruel we become? Why do we hate or dislike the difference?

G-d in his eternal wisdom created changes for us not to be bored of each other and enjoy the difference.

Imagine if he had created all women as beautiful blonds with blue eyes. I promise you wouldn't leave your house if he had done so: you would become bored of looking at them.

Each time I saw life in Gaza I prayed harder for peace and harmony.

These frequent overseas trips not only didn't help
my marriage any but rather made it worse. The result was
a major depression causing a breakdown. I didn't want to
get out of bed, with suicidal tendencies.

This was coupled with the Iranian revolution of 1979,
which made me feel worse. I loved Iran and was worried
for what maybe would come next in that country. What
bothered me was not the revolution but rather the hard
years any revolution brings with itself. A revolution in Iran
was long overdue.

The Shah had wanted to westernize Iran at any cost.
The country had belonged to the so called "thousand
families," a small percentage of people who lived like
lords while the rest of the country struggled to survive.
There were even some who sold their blood on Friday
mornings to buy food for their families (I am a witness).

The Shah had become a megalomaniac with
dictatorial behavior (it is true that he had been
disappointed by those close to him soon becoming flies in
search of sweets) to the point that he had convinced
himself of his divine purpose on Earth.

Among his major mistakes there might be at least two
worthy of mention.

First, he had fought religion and the clergy. It is
surprising that the Shah had not learned from world
history.

No leader in history has ever fought religion and won.

All in all, he had no reason to fight religion. Why in an
Islamic country we had to see miniskirts? Why there
would be liquor shops on every street?

Didn't he think that Iran didn't have nor wanted the same
pattern of behavior of the western world? Was the western
world sharing the developments in science and

industry with Iran or was it that the land was a dumping ground for their goods and vanities?

His next mistake was the way he conducted the white revolution. The analphabet farmers first needed to be conditioned and trained before overwhelming them with freedom from their feudal masters. This was the reason why his white revolution didn't work out.

History shows how some free slaves, after the American Civil War, came back to their prior masters seeking jobs.

Freedom must be step by step for someone who has lived in oppression all his life. We saw the same when the Almighty took the Jewish slaves out of Egypt to lead them to the Promised Land. A destination reachable within three months took forty years. Why? Perhaps one of his reasons was that he simply wanted fresh blood without any complexes entering a new land.

In a final attempt to revive my marriage I approached my wife asking what could be done to have another chance.

She eagerly accepted my proposal when I said I shall separate from my brothers as long as she helps me in the business hand in hand. She agreed.

The separation from my brothers was painful but a necessary step in saving my home.

We ended up with several stores and a wholesale operation in New York.

To my dismay, my wife soon changed her mind in helping me saying it was too late to mend the wounds.

I no longer was in touch with reality. I was not functioning.

I was down and out.

As fate would have it, it was a man from my own ghetto who saved my life.

He was Rabbi Doctor Dayan. A clinical psychologist who came to my help. I was under his care for over two years before I stopped having migraine headaches and depressions.

My business, all around, was failing due to absentee management except the wholesale operation. I couldn't help but notice the large amounts it was selling to Puerto Rican boutiques. They came to New York in search of large quantities of clothing.

I fell in love with nature when I took a short trip to San Juan. I could easily justify the fact that Puerto Rico was called "the enchanted island"—it was nature at its best.

Soon Puerto Rico was among my destinations when traveling. There, I found simplicity, nature and tranquility not found in over-civilized cities. People were warm and enjoyed life one day at a time.

Not before long, I had a boutique in one of the best Puerto Rican shopping centers. It was quite successful at first but started lagging behind due to absentee management. This had become the story of my life namely having great business spots in many places without proper supervision.

Soon I had to declare bankruptcy and close down everything except one store in Miami and the one in Puerto Rico.

It dawned on me one afternoon when I was reading a book by Anton Chekhov that my life had to change.

Enough was enough. I remembered the words of my psychologist telling me: "You would have been freed by now had you been a hard criminal." I needed a change of life away from it all.

I packed my suitcase and informed my wife of my departure no knowing if or when I would be back. I promised her to see to my financial responsibilities both to her as well as to my children, who were off to different colleges.

I had gone through hell and back with the dream of America, America and yet now was about to leave it.

How ironic. I had achieved in America what most American-borns never achieve and yet I was a failure.

I left Miami, with a heavy heart, for San Juan, exchanging four houses for a rented wooden room on the roof of a house which was waiting to be my domicile.

# Chapter 22

# New life in Puerto Rico

# Chapter 22

## New life in Puerto Rico

Next morning when I arrived at the store, there was chaos. Inventory was low with unpaid debts of about seven thousand dollars.

There was no chance of filling the store with credit due to declaration of my bankruptcy. Everything had to be bought with cash. How much could a man take? I had left one trouble spot to arrive at another.

What happened next was none but the work of skies.

John Regis, a successful businessman who had bought a store from me years ago in Miami, suddenly appeared in my life again. He was an angel without wings sent from above. Once again the Almighty was pulling me up before I was down and out. He was interested in buying the store for a new project he had in mind. He paid me more than the boutique was worth. We entered a contract based on a handshake.

Half of what he paid me was sent to my wife to pay our debts as well as house and college expenses of the children.

Due to my bankruptcy, I didn't need to pay any debts but there was the question of my conscience. My suppliers had trusted me, they were my friends.

A new venture was inevitable since there was no income. Yet I no longer wanted to have anything to do with clothing. What I had gone through with boutiques was enough for a lifetime.

Fast food seemed a good idea. The asset manager of the mall who knew of my troubles suggested a small store in a very visible corner of the food court. The lease was signed while the main question remained: what to sell?

After canvassing the island, the main idea came from a countryside vegetable market: fresh fruit shakes. (Later this was copied from me to the point each mall had at least a kiosk devoted to fresh fruit shakes.) Fruit shake didn't seem enough since it was to be a fast food.

Hours on end I stood in front of different food outlets taking notes and pictures. Typical sandwiches were the answer.

The store was built, equipment bought and all was ready to go. For now, I could only hire one person as cashier while I was the cook and the server. In the name of G-d I opened the counter.

Wow. The store ran out of food by three in the afternoon.

Months before when John had seen me in depression, he had told me soon I will be smiling. He was right. I was now smiling. Soon more people were hired to help but I still worked from early morning to eight in the evening. It was exciting. It was physical work. My mind was taking a break.

A good amount of money was sent home every month for all expenses. As for me, it was all work except Saturday nights.

I didn't know any people to socialize with. Going to a casino was the Saturday routine. It wasn't enough.

From time to time, I would meet a pretty lady at the mall whom I took to dinner on the weekends. There was no guilt feeling anymore. I was separated from my wife.

Driving around the countryside admiring nature and wishing I had a piece of land to farm became a habit.

All in all, people were warm and friendly. They enjoyed my Spanish accent and admired me for being a

216

foreigner working so many hours without any complaint.

One day, standing by the counter, I saw Carlos passing by. He was a friend from Fordham Road in the Bronx where I had a boutique. At the time, he managed a shoe store next to my shop. What a coincidence that was!

He had been sent to Puerto Rico by a chain store which had had not been a success and eventually had to close down. He was looking for a job. He was an honest man. At my suggestion, he started looking at failing food stores. The idea was to get hold of such establishments and revive them.

We took the first store (with all equipment left behind) at a slow mall and opened a Pizzeria. We had opened three stores at the same center within six months. Money was rolling in.

It was on a Sunday afternoon when walking out of the store for a coffee break when I saw a beautiful blond lady with sad green eyes sitting at a table a few feet away.

With uncontrolled knees, I approached her:

"Good afternoon, dear lady."

Before she had a chance to answer, I asked her why such beautiful eyes look so sad.

She smiled. "Hi, my name is Marilyn." I couldn't help but see the tears in her eyes. She signaled me to sit next to her asking me who I was. Where am I from? My answer to her was that I am a wandering man in search of tranquility and relative happiness.

She turned out to have four children with an unhappy marriage. In fact, she went as far as saying that she is separated from her husband while still living together under the same roof. When I asked her why she went on saying she was an evangelist, a church member who didn't want to hurt her children or her parents through a divorce.

Our conversation lasted for a long time. It seemed we had known each other by the time she left.

A few days later, she called to wish me a happy birthday. She asked whether she could pass by to wish me well in person.

I was glad. I really wanted to see her again knowing well that I could not have more than a platonic relationship with a married woman even if I wanted to. There was no need to become a bigger sinner.

The day she came to see me, I truly thought someone had given life to a "Barbie doll." She looked amazing. Not only that her eyes no longer were sad looking, but rather shining like a pair of Colombian emeralds.

The lady wanted to know if there is job opening at the shop.

Realizing she was a church goer coupled with the need of an honest person to be in charge of sales whenever I went to check other businesses, I said yes without any hesitation.

I was falling in love. It was wrong.

At my request, I met her husband who turned out to be a very educated and kind man. Presenting myself, I truly tried to mend their relationship. After all, I had done so before in Hong Kong when my supplier, at the time, had left his wife and children for a model. He had been so grateful to me he had told me "You now have a brother in Hong Kong."

I tried on three occasions to make peace between the two of them but had no success.

Marilyn or Tata (her nickname) took me every weekend to the countryside where she helped me rent a room for weekends. More and more I was falling in love with the beauty of this enchanted island. The only thing making me sad or think was lack of farmed land. Everything was imported from the USA!!!

Ever since a child, I had always enjoyed planting and gardening. Perhaps now there was a chance to materialize my dream. I wanted a farm.

Soon, through Tata's help, I had the pleasure of meeting an evangelist pastor (a true man of peace and love who went out of his way to help anyone who needed help) who helped me find six acres of land right in front of the magical rainforest El Yunque. What a panorama! I don't think a panorama as such could even be found in Utopia. It was majestic. It still is.

In the morning one could swear manna is falling from the sky in the shape of white cloud while at sundown one might easily believe the mountain is on fire.

Two years down the road and with Tata's help we planted hundreds of typical fruit trees of the region as well as devoting time to minor vegetables.

A small house was built on the farm with the hope that my children would come as often as possible. After all this was their farm.

I was getting to have patriotic feelings about the island.

It was distressing to see most produce came from stateside.

Why couldn't Puerto Rico farm and plant?

I gathered statistical data and framed it showing it on the counter at every one of my shops. I went as far wearing a t-shirt with the famous words of a well- known Puerto Rican writer on the front: Conio Boriqua Despiertate. Which, politely put, meant: Come on, Puerto Rican, wake up.

It was clear that as long as there were the so called US handouts and no help from the local government, the island could not stand on its feet. The food coupons were spent on American produce. So what was it? Was America helping the Puerto Rican? Or was it protecting the American farmer's income?

It all turned out that I can only protect the land and worry about it as an individual and no more.

Another interesting event worth mentioning is when during one of my Sunday lectures on topics from the Old Testament I met Mr. Scott. He was an elderly man with a thick German accent which made me think that he might be an ex-Nazi hiding in Puerto Rico. I made investigations of him for about three months. which resulted in my being ashamed of myself.

It turned out that he had escaped with his parents from Germany in the thirties to America. Soon after getting a degree in music he had put himself at the service of the poor and the orphans on the Island. He had turned out to be an evangelist and a man of G-d. We became the best of friends till he passed away in 2002.

It had been over a year since Tata had gotten a divorce from her husband. We were very affectionate with each other but marriage was out of question for a few reasons.

Her children had been deeply hurt by the divorce and I wasn't about to aggravate them further.

Next, our strong cultural differences coupled with the fact that I had failed in the institution of marriage kept me away from marrying again.

There is no denying that she took care of me and was the only one who worried about my wellbeing. We were very close to each other but she was disappointed at my decision against marriage.

It was at a concert that I met Fred. He was the Dean of the Faculty of Food and Alimentation at the University. He also suffered knowing that Puerto Rico wasn't self-sufficient. He was very disturbed that, for example, oranges go to waste on the island while orange juice is imported from elsewhere.

Suddenly an idea was born. I was going to open a juice company and also acquire a license to sell water.

Fred took me to the University laboratories teaching me all he could about juice making.

I opened a juice company with second hand equipment and tried my products under the rules of the health department first at our own stores. The reception was great. No less than this was expected since we used real fruits to make our juices.

Soon our fresh orange juice as well as other fruit juices was replacing Tropicana and other companies in the four and five star hotels, Fred and I were jumping for joy. We had proved "YES WE CAN."

Everything was looking up. Tata reluctantly had accepted our relationship. She was content but not completely happy with the status quo.

Many a time I had heard of Murphy's Law (when nothing should go wrong, something usually does). I was about to experience this law now first hand.

A gas explosion in the vicinity of where Carlos and I had three stores resulted in structural damage as well as in fatalities.

This was enough to convert a lucrative area into a ghost house. We had to close down our shops within a few months.

Unfortunately, when it rains it pours. The sandwich shop, my flagship, was losing ground fast due to an illogical decision:

this was the only shopping center which decided to have two or more outlets of the same fast food in the food court.

It got even rainier when Hurricane George devastated the eastern part of the island where we had the juice factory.

It didn't calculate. Nothing made sense. I went as far as believing the cause could be an evil eye. From night to day, I had become poor again from no fault of mine.

It was a few weeks after the hurricane when I almost lost my life to the assailant who had tried to hold me up.

That event single handedly made me feel worse than anything. It took me several weeks till through logic and deduction I found the man and had him arrested.

For the next four years, I single handedly ran the sandwich shop, which hardly gave me an income, till finally it was sold at a fraction of what it was worth.

Once again it was new day, new life. Trying my best to find a job was futile. With great hardship, I opened a new store but had to close it down since my depressions no longer allowed me to be very rational.

Puerto Rico had become my new home. I was in heaven whenever I worked on the farm yet I had failed again. True it hadn't been my fault but that was the reality.

It was my youngest daughter and her husband who came to my help. They suggested I move to Fort Lauderdale where they will find me a job.

The decision was made then. Before leaving, I called Tata to the side assuring her that she owes me nothing. I told her she would be free to make any decision she needed to make but also promised not to forget her and travel to the island as often as possible.

# Chapter 23

# Back to Florida

An artisan at work in the bazar - Esfahan

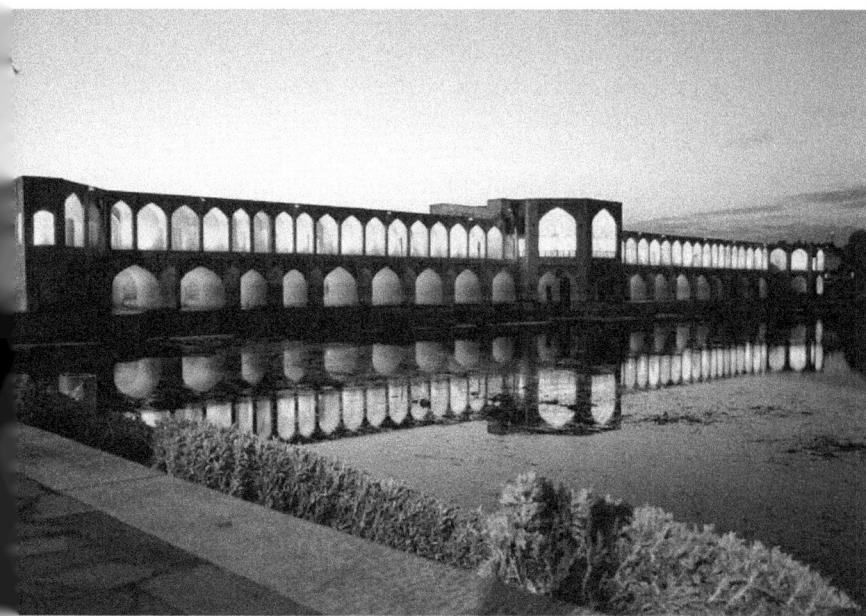

Sio Sepol- The thirty three bridge - Esfahan

# Chapter 23

# Back to Florida

Fort Lauderdale looked to me quite different in 2002 as compared with when I had left twelve years ago.

My son in law got me a job as collector in a bank for nine dollars an hour. I was grateful to him. I had no more ambitions left in me. So a simple job was most adequate although not very rewarding financially.

My entire time was devoted to the new job except Friday nights and Sundays, which I happily spent with my two grandchildren.

My income grew hand in hand with my extra duties. It took about two years till I became an executive manager with a portfolio of over one hundred million under my care.

Buying a one bedroom apartment in a senior community was cheaper than paying rent. Tata was coming to see me now when possible while I went to the island two to three times a year just to work and lose myself on the farm.

Somehow eight years of management was enough. The anxiety was becoming too much. It was time to make the load on my back lighter.

Approaching the higher echelon of the company and at my request, I relinquished my position in favor of a lower paying job without management responsibilities.

This was two years ago when I turned sixty six. I now work six months in Fort Lauderdale, while the other six months is spent working as a gentleman farmer on the farm. Hopefully, 2014 will be the last year at work.

I can hardly wait to be on the farm all year round.

When I reflect on my life evaluating all that I have gone through it brings me but to a few points.

Life is short and a passage, confirming the wise
words of King Solomon "Vanity of vanities, all is
vanity." As well, there is nothing new under the sun and
nothing is forever.

Again as the wise Solomon said: blessed is the man
who lived life to the fullest and walked in the path of G-d.

Do I consider myself a failure? No, a thousand times no.
I have been to many countries and lived in some, which is
more than many accomplish during a lifetime.

Above all, I have been blessed with good children
and sweet grandchildren. What more could I ask for?

And now in the autumn of my years, I shall be
content with whatever may be next. I am happy with my
lot.

Among many things I have learned one comes out on
the top.

Those of us who leave our countries in search of a
better life might do better in the long run if we were only
willing to work in the native country as hard as we would
be willing to work elsewhere.

Who am I?

How I wish the following words were mine. But
they are not. So allow me to borrow them from
Mahatma Gandhi: "I am a Jew, a Christian and a
Muslim." I also respect all religions which promote
goodness and love of fellow human beings.

Love thy neighbor as thyself.

# Chapter 24

# Enough, enough, enough

# Chapter 24

# Enough, enough, enough

I write the following words as an individual; as a member of the human race. I mean no offence to any group or establishment.

IRAN and IRANIANS—they are not Arabs but Persian.

A vast land of beauty blessed by nature with all the natural resources a country might wish to have. As for the inhabitants, let us just say that one will hardly find another nation as hospitable as the Iranians. How sad then when we look back and see how the western world's greed has caused Iran misery and troubles. Iranians are not warriors and leave violence as the last effort. In this, they very much follow the steps of the Prophet, who considered arms bearing as a final alternative. Iran is the land of the world's greatest poetry and not the land of war mongers.

Iran, together with some other countries, is angry. Angry, due to its exploitations by foreign powers for centuries.

Nevertheless, Iran, an Islamic land, does not seek wars but tries to remind the mighty powers about justice.

The Islam I learned and admired was through its followers (my teachers, my friends, my Boy Scout leaders). I learned from them to be generous and

Forgiving, to search for knowledge and never forget the poor.

Often, people criticize the Iranian life based on Islamic laws and tradition. Does it have to adopt the western values to be accepted?

Occidental traditions, culture and laws may be perfect and I am sure they are, but for the Occident; they should not be imposed on others.

Those who criticize Iran for human rights will do well to look at their own surroundings to see whether they themselves follow what is asked of others.

As for women's rights, it was the Prophet who abolished the killing of baby girls at birth (prior to abolishment, baby girls were killed so that they wouldn't be stolen by other tribes once adolescent).

It was Islam that made laws to protect the woman and women's rights and respect. Another reason why a woman has a revered position in Islam is due to the fact that half of the religion is learned from a mother.

In addition, Iran has no reason to attack any country in the area for further land or glory. It might have been a correct theory during the reign of the Shah who suffered of grandiosity and perhaps even had eyes on emirates around the Gulf, but not today's Iran.

Like all other countries of the world, Iran has her own problems to solve. It is not an easy task to provide a future for over two-thirds of the population, who are under the age thirty. Knowing that oil reserves are not forever, it is not easy to find an alternative overnight.

Yes, she wants to see justice, peace and harmony in the Middle East and should also realize that helping to arm groups will only aggravate the situation since violence begets violence.

Iran, like any other country, has the right to atomic energy in accordance with the pertinent international

Laws. Therefore, she should not be victimized by double standards.

Yes, Iran by all means wants to see peace and justice in the Middle East but not by means of a nuclear war.

Iranians are among the most intelligent around. They well know the consequences of such war in the region, the least of all the possibility of having radioactive oil not suitable to use for decades or more. The best weapon at hand and the only one is communication.

In the case of an all out war on Iran, the consequences will be such that in comparison, the wars in Afghanistan and Iraq will look like a piece of cake. An all war out against Iran, in the case of its success, will bring about many factions in the land who will not necessarily stay within the Iranian borders but rather might become a terrible cause for turmoil for the Emirates, Kuwait, and Saudis as well as for other neighboring lands.

It would be advisable to get to know Iran and the Iranians not by sensationalism but by interaction and real means before one decides to love or hate her.

The ISRAELI-PALESTINIAN dilemma

Israel was never left without Jewish inhabitants unless they were taken away as slaves by Assyrians, Babylonians and Romans. And even then, most would return to the land once those mighty empires were no more.

The only conqueror showing compassion and offering total freedom was the great King Cyrus of Persia (Iran) who even offered assistance so Jews could rebuild Jerusalem. He championed human rights 2500 years ago.

His kindness was so great that when he conquered Babylonia and freed the Jews most went back with him to Persia, settling in Sepahan, today's Esfahan.

The Jewish sorrow of our time started well before the Second World War when Jews perished in "pogroms" (attacking of Jewish villages, mostly in Russia, killing, raping and vandalizing under the context of being Christ killers).

Jews were victimized for any reason that could be found including the accusation that they killed Christian children to use their blood in Matzo for Passover.

Once Communism appeared on the scene, some young people left for Palestine where they established co-operative farms and lived next to their Arab cousins in peace.

The Second World War changed the scenery. Millions were killed and the fraction of Jews who survived were homeless and in shock. Some might say, but some 60 million perished, how come the Jewish Holocaust remains at the center? This argument has validity, but in the case of the Jews, a program was set to annihilate a whole race and that is why it is different.

Neither during the war nor after did anyone want the Jews, or care, with the exception of the Danes, the Dutch and some angelic gentiles who actually endangered their lives to save Jews.

But they were few. When President Roosevelt was asked for permission to bomb the concentration camps his answer was "No let's finish the war first and then we will free the Jews."

In other words, so what if another million or two are burnt till then!

How about the "ship of the damned" when Hitler set a thousand Jews afloat to emigrate elsewhere?

Neither Cuba, America nor Canada admitted them, forcing the ship back, where most of its passengers perished in the concentration camps.

The survivors had no place to go but to Palestine.

Skirmishes commenced between Arabs and Jews till the United Nations partition of Palestine in 1947 when each was given a part of the land. It was on May 15 1948 that Prime Minister Ben-Gurion declared independence.

Within hours surrounding Arab countries attacked the new state of Israel while blasting over their radios inviting the Palestinian Arabs to join in, in order to push the Jews to the sea.

Many left to join the Arab armies while those who stayed put were given Israeli citizenship.

Many years and more than enough wars have not resolved the discord between Palestinians and Israelis.

Time and again, countries have tried to broker a peace with no definite success.

The only relevant parties to put an end to this dilemma are the two sides themselves and no one else. They simply must continue to communicate with each other regardless of the amount of time it takes till both get tired. There is a saying in Spanish and quite appropriate to mention here. "No hay mal que dure cien años ni cuerpo que lo aguante" (There is no sickness which could last a hundred years nor a body which could tolerate it).

We have already seen where wars and violence have not offered any benefit.

Israel and Jews have a moral obligation to help the Palestinian issue by trying their best. Why? Because a race having come close to annihilation must extend its hands in helping those in distress.

It is bizarre that both sides have forgotten about their real enemy—demography.

235

The land is small and is over populated. Soon there won't be enough space to house either party. It might be a good idea to curtail the rate of birth on both sides.

They say reality starts with dreams. Let me dream then.

What if the Palestinians had the occupied lands plus a small piece of Sinai Desert as well as a small piece of Jordanian desert land? Let Israel take care of its infrastructure. Then maybe the cousins could live in peace next to each other.

As for Jerusalem, it could and perhaps should become an international city.

Every human being has the right to a piece of bread, a shirt on his back and a roof to keep him from the rain.

This is a G-d given right.

Those of us fortunate enough should not stop aiding the Palestinians with food, medicine and education till the problematic issues are resolved.


AMERICA. A promised land?


This blessed land was supposed to be the last frontier of hope for those persecuted and distressed. Has it changed? Perhaps.

We claim "in G-d we trust." I wonder! Is our trust in Him or in the greenback? Are we behaving as the forefathers had planned or is it that we are becoming decadent, greedy and arrogant? We preach righteously to the rest of the world while we don't practice same at home.

Democracy is being abused on all levels and yet we try our best to export this regime to the rest of the world.

Why is it that we cannot comprehend the fact that democracy must be tailor made with the religion, culture and traditions of each land? Thus, what we call democracy might not be suitable elsewhere.

Why do we act as the international police force? Are we really a nation of war mongers?

America screams at other countries preaching human rights!!!

Can anyone tell me, in good faith, equality between black and white America exists even today when we have an African American president?

As for American generosity, which is riding on the back of the middle class America, it is another bizarre subject.

We leave our old and poor here at home with problems while sending assistance to the outside world.

Let us light up the house before we light the church.

And when we finally assist others let it be that we teach them how to fish rather than sending them a fish.

America absorbs the best of every land in all fields, particularly in sciences. Rather than exporting decadence and the wrong messages, let us export medicine and other scientific finds which could help a given country stand on its own feet.

Looking back at the history, it could clearly be seen that great empires were destroyed by their own doing. It would be ungodly if this were allowed to happen in America.

Should we need to wage another war as we did in Iraq, where we could have easily done away with Saddam Hussein and a few others to free the country, let it not be the case where we killed a cow for the sake of a glass of milk.

America is the last frontier of hope. Let's take care of it in a responsible manner without arrogance and in good faith.

ENOUGH, ENOUGH, ENOUGH

We have all had enough of wars and miseries brought about by ourselves in every corner of this Earth.

How I wish I could run to the streets of the world screaming at all governments and at the racists: "Enough, enough, and enough."

The human race has enough wars to fight against natural disasters without adding man-made problems. Let us all hand in hand find ways to fight hurricanes, tsunamis, earthquakes and more.

Until "the string theory" can provide us directions to another planet like ours, this beautiful Earth is all we have.

We owe it to our children.

Let us fight hunger in the world without selfishness so that we no longer look at a picture taken by a photojournalist depicting a vulture standing near a dying African baby, out of hunger, waiting to devour its skin and bones once the baby is dead.

ENOUGH          ENOUGH          ENOUGH

Khaju Bridge in Esfahan